Hartlepool Borough Libraries

This book is issued for four **3** weeks and should be returned on or before this date. It may, if not required by another reader, be renewed on request for a further four **3** weeks.

Please telephone Central Library on 01429 272905 to renew.

And will you succeed? Yes! You will, indeed! (98 and ¾ per cent guaranteed.) Kid, you'll move mountains.

Dr. Seuss, *Oh, The Places You'll Go!*

From Ordinary to Extraordinary

How to Live an Exceptional Life

BRIAN COLBERT

Gill & Macmillan

Gill & Macmillan
Hume Avenue
Park West
Dublin 12
with associated companies throughout the world
www.gillmacmillanbooks.ie

978 07171 5292 6

Print origination by O'K Graphic Design, Dublin
Printed and bound by CPI Group (UK) Ltd, Croydon, CR0 4YY

This book is typeset in Officina Sans 10.5/13 pt

The paper used in this book comes from the wood pulp of managed forests. For every tree felled, at least one tree is planted, thereby renewing natural resources.

A CIP catalogue record for this book is available from the British Library.

Note: All NLP tools and techniques are used with the expressed consent of Richard Bandler and John La Valle.

Dedication

To Mum, who taught me to be different.

To Dad, who taught me how to see the funny side.

To my wife Theresa, you are extraordinary!

About the Author

Brian Colbert is a motivational speaker and is regarded as one of the most prominent and successful mind coaches in Ireland today. Brian has qualifications and many years of experience in the social sciences, along with twenty years of experience in industrial relations and personnel management. However, he credits most of his success to his use of Neuro-Linguistic Programming (NLP). He is a licensed Master Trainer of NLP and co-founder of the Irish Institute of NLP. Brian features regularly on television and radio, and in print media.

CONTENTS

About your *Mind of Genius* CD

The attached CD is designed to help you to get the most out of your mind and boost your creativity as you work your way through the book. It is a hypnotic CD and, as such, you must avoid driving or engaging in any other activities while using it.

You can listen to the CD as often as you like; ideally once a day for the first twenty-one days and as often as you like thereafter. If you find you enjoy the CD, there are plenty of similar ones available for you to try. Visit www.briancolbert.ie for more details.

Acknowledgments

It takes a lot of people for a book to make it to the shelves. I would like to thank everyone who has helped me or who has been a source of inspiration. I particularly want to thank Richard Bandler, John Grinder and Robert Dilts, whose work has truly changed the world.

Thanks to Michael Connolly for helping me to bounce my ideas. Thanks to Owen Fitzpatrick: we still have more good stuff to do. Thanks to my sons Dylan and Cian for their creative input and advice. Thanks to Karen Keating and Niamh Fitzpatrick.

My sincere thanks to Fergal Tobin, Nicki Howard, Catherine Gough, Emma Farrell and all the team at Gill & Macmillan, whose level of professionalism exudes excellence.

A great, big, huge thanks to my wife Theresa, for keeping the show on the road and for her incredible tolerance, support and patience right the way through.

Enjoy!

Brian

Introduction

Let me ask you to indulge yourself for a moment and think of a time when you well and truly impressed yourself. A time when perhaps you were up against it but you made it through – and with flying colours, too. When you think about it, you did pretty well. Actually, if you are to be honest about it you were downright legendary! You know that feeling – when you come to the realisation that you have actually done it. There's always that slight hesitation before your subdued smile suddenly shifts to an enormous grin and brightens up your whole face. Your eyes sparkle with delight and your heart fills with pride. A sudden surge of playfulness engages your whole body, making you want to throw your hands in the air and do a little jig for yourself. You feel like shouting from the rooftops: 'Yes, Yes, Yes, Yes, YES! Oh, YES! You *did* it! You *nailed* it! You *got* it! Ladies and gentlemen, please be upstanding … '

Ok, so perhaps they weren't your exact words but you know what I am talking about. You know that feeling. That is the feeling of being extraordinary. And while we can't be extraordinary *all* of the time, wouldn't it be nice to be extraordinary a lot *more* of the time? What if I said you could have many more of those moments in your life? What if I was to tell you that you could stack the cards in your favour? What if there were things you could learn that would practically *guarantee* more of those experiences?

Here's the thing: becoming extraordinary involves learning some rules. Life is subject to natural laws that hold things in place in this world. It is the failure to correctly apply these laws that causes the most limitation in life. To improve, you need to fully understand and fully engage with these laws. Throughout history, extraordinary people have mastered this ability. They understood the universal laws. They worked within these laws. They expressed these laws in their lives in the manner in which they saw fit. Some of them amassed great wealth; some of them came up with great inventions; and some of them produced great works of art. Some of them were religious gurus; some were entrepreneurs; others were known simply as 'genius'. It didn't matter what time and place these people were born into. Muhammad Ali, Bill Gates, Leonardo da Vinci, Oprah Winfrey, Albert Einstein ... all of these people have made their mark in the world in some way.

There are so many extraordinary people who feature in this book. In writing about them, I hope to demonstrate that the qualities of extraordinary people are underpinned by certain behaviours, skills and attitudes – all of which can be *learned*. I have drawn from disciplines such as psychology, sociology, Shamanism, Taoism, Buddhism and NLP. The worlds of physics, systems theory, field theory and even maths are explored. The common threads are human potential and the search for maximum self-expression.

Of course, the real icing on the cake is that this stuff is actually easy. With just a little effort, you can apply these things in your own life. You can develop your social, mental and creative fitness. You can be free from unnecessary distractions. You can live your life on your own terms. You can extract excitement and magic from days that might have been ordinary. You can realise your potential and reach new heights of excellence. You can bring from within yourself all that you are capable of becoming. You can express yourself in the way you want. You can get from life everything that you have dreamed of. You can be successful – and I mean finding success as *you* define it, finding peak performance in whatever *you* decide is worthwhile. You can become the master or mistress of your own universe!

You are about to learn how to use your mind with great precision. You are about to learn the tools that will help you to program your mind for success. You will learn how to use language, verbal and non-verbal, for greater effect. You will learn how to predict and influence your own behaviour and the behaviour of others. You will learn how to build great relationships. You will learn how to handle those relationships that are a challenge. You will discover how to motivate, inspire and guide yourself and others on the path to becoming extraordinary.

This book is about your mind, your heart and your soul. This book digs deeper so that you can travel further. This book shows you what works. This book reminds you that you are powerful beyond measure. This book affirms that you can *be* the change you want to see in the world. This book invites you to be part of something bigger. This is a book about revolution *and* evolution.

This book will teach you extraordinary skills; how you *apply* them is entirely up to you. Whether you choose to be a rock star or a rising star makes no difference: *you* get to write the script. You live in a world of abundant possibility. You live in a world that is wide open to your influence. It is a world that, in my opinion, could do with bigger and better dreams. This world is hungry for creative thought and input. *Now* is the time for fresh thinking, new ideas and a greater sense of respect and passion. I hope that you find all of these things and more in this book. Use it to become everything that you want to be. *Become extraordinary.* If you do this, you change the whole world. Why? Because we are all connected; each of us is made of the same stuff. What happens to one of us affects all of us. We share a common destiny. We are all made of the same matter. And *that* is what matters the most.

CHAPTER 1

The Path of the Extraordinary

All the evidence that we have indicates that it is reasonable to assume in practically every human being, certainly in almost every newborn baby, that there is an active will toward health, an impulse toward growth, or toward the actualization of human potentialities.

Abraham Maslow

Most of us are intrigued by the lives of the rich and famous. We like to get a look in, put ourselves in their shoes and wonder what it would be like if we were in their role. This interest extends itself to celebrities and successful people from all walks of life. There are articles, books and magazines filled with 'How I made it to the top' stories. We read, we study, we pick up tips and we might even apply a few; but we rarely seem to get as far as we would like. 'You have to have what it takes', 'You need to work hard to succeed'; we have heard it all before and we will hear it again. We love rags-to-riches stories but deep down we believe them to be the exception rather than the rule. There appears to be something missing: that ever-elusive X-factor, that secret ingredient that makes all the difference. Is it belief? Is it luck? Is it genetic? Is it IQ, EQ or sucking up to HQ? Whatever it is, it seems to be out of our reach. In the end, some of us settle for fascination with the lives of others. We spend our time being bystanders, instead of making our *own* lives something worth envying.

If you want to be the best you can be, if you want to reach your full potential, then it makes sense to study those who have already reached theirs. Obviously, each person will have their own take on things, so what is needed is a system that covers the overall process rather than individual idiosyncrasies. In NLP (Neuro-Linguistic Programming) we call this process *modelling*.

First, we will look at the process that leads to living an exceptional life. As we do so, we will explore the obstacles and distractions that stand in the way of you realising your highest ambitions, the things that cause inconsistencies and the reasons why there are more ordinary than extraordinary days in your life. Think of this as the time to tilt the balance back in your favour.

Once we have done this, we can come up with a working model that combines the qualities of peak performance, genius, self-actualization and enlightenment. In working with this model, I will demonstrate how you can generate the skills required of it. This will give you the ability and the scope to add so much more sparkle to your life. And so, you can begin to live the life you were born to live!

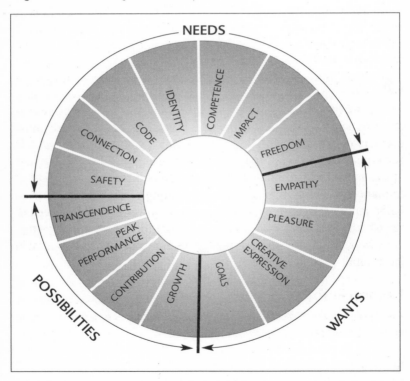

The Wheel of Human Potential

Examine the chart above. It points towards the fact that we have to satisfy our survival needs before we can meet other needs. Our most basic needs include food, shelter, warmth and reproduction. Alongside these needs there are, in my opinion, further needs that are just as important. In my first book, *The Happiness Habit*, I addressed these core needs as Human Fulfilment Drives. To place them in a wider context in this book, I will reframe them as *Human Fulfilment Needs*. These are the critical needs that we are driven to satisfy no matter what. These needs reflect the human experience at its most basic. They drive our behaviour and occupy our attention. If they are absent, we seek them. We are out of balance without them. They are the 'must-haves', the 'non-negotiables' without which we fail to function at the most basic level of normality. These needs offer the backdrop to our core values and set the tone of our fundamental perceptions of life.

In addition to the Human Fulfilment Needs are *Human Fulfilment Wants*. While they aren't critical for survival, they play a vital role in our psychological and emotional health. A well-adjusted human being will satisfy their Human Fulfilment Wants.

Beyond the Human Fulfilment Wants are *Human Fulfilment Possibilities*. These are what make us extraordinary. We can live perfectly good lives without these possibilities, but living with them energises our life experience and takes it to a whole new level. This is the shift from ordinary to extraordinary! It is not something you have to do but it is something that is well worth doing. When you get even the slightest hint of this move towards the extraordinary, perhaps during a moment of brilliance, your life bathes in the enchanting afterglow. The Human Fulfilment Possibilities are the high hanging fruits. You may need to stretch a little to reach them but the sweetest fruits are always at the top.

Now let's explore every element of the Wheel of Human Potential in more detail.

Human Fulfilment Needs

There are seven Human Fulfilment Needs: safety, connection, code, identity, competence, impact and freedom.

Safety

Each of us feels the need to be safe. Safety comes when you know there will be enough food on the table, the bills can be paid and you can put your head to the pillow without having to worry about what is going to happen next.

Connection
We all want to love and be loved. We want to be accepted, respected and validated by our chosen groups, tribes or communities.

Code
Whether we choose to break them or not, we need to know that there are rules and guidelines. This gives us a sense of certainty and balance in the world. Our codes reflect the boundaries, standards and beliefs to which we hold ourselves (and others) accountable and answerable.

Identity
As much as we need to know what the rules are, we also need to know *who we are* and what we stand for. A person's identity is made up of all seven Human Fulfilment Needs.

Competence
Each of us has an inbuilt need to be good at something and to be known for this competence. This gives us a sense of recognition and validation.

Impact
The scriptwriter Leo Rosten once wrote: 'I cannot believe that the purpose of life is to be happy ... the purpose of life is ... to matter, to count, to stand for something, to have made some difference that you lived at all.' To be good at something is one thing; to be good *for* something is quite another. Each of us needs to know that we are important, significant and needed in some way. We need to know that who we are and what we do counts for something.

Freedom
In my opinion, being free and *feeling* free are horses of a different colour. Few people want total freedom because being free like that means not being attached to anything, which goes against our need for connection. However, we do need to feel free to come and go as we please within reason. Freedom is a balancing act and we are all prepared to give up certain freedoms for the sake of meeting other social needs.

Summary
Human Fulfilment Needs tend to operate progressively. When our need for safety is met, this gives rise to the need for connection, which in turn

leads to a need for code, and so on. Over time, these needs work simultaneously and become interdependent. For example, if a person loses their job, they will lose a number of things at once. They may go through the following thought process:

I am being made redundant.
Safety: What am I going to do for money now?
Connection: There goes the weekends out with the lads.
Impact: I guess nobody appreciates good craftsmanship anymore.
Competence: Who is going to employ me now? This is all I know how to do.
Code: I guess there's nothing more I can do.
Freedom: I'll have to tighten the belt, put a load of things on hold and just sit it out until things get better.
Identity: Right now this all feels like a big blur. I don't know what end of me is up. I mean, I don't know whether I'm coming or going. I don't know. I just don't know ...

The above thought process takes you through an assault on the seven Human Fulfilment Needs. When a person loses their job, their feeling of safety is affected. Their feeling of connection may also be affected. When both of these needs are hit, this may bring about a questioning of identity. The problem will be exasperated if work is the place where the individual feels they make an impact and express their competence. If that person is the sole earner in the household, you can be sure that their freedom will be severely restricted because of losing their job.

If a person fails to restore this balance, they could feel helpless, hopeless and worthless over time. This is a real challenge to their sense of humanity and it is not a healthy state of mind for anyone to occupy. Balance is needed. In this case, re-employment is certainly a solution but there are other ways of restoring balance. All effort and attention now naturally shifts to meeting these Human Fulfilment Needs. This will happen with or without conscious intent, since the person is now in survival mode. Even if the person remains unemployed, over time their life will show evidence of these needs being met elsewhere. Perhaps they will volunteer for charity work, help their neighbours or take on some DIY projects. Regardless of what goes on in our lives, at all times we are either meeting these Human Fulfilment Needs or working towards meeting them.

Exercise: Assessment of Human Fulfilment Needs

Here is an example of one person's assessment of their need for impact.

Need	How are you meeting this need?	What more can you do?
Impact	Being the best mum I can be	Become a life coach
	Helping out at a community centre	
	Teaching the kids to write stories	

Assess how each of the Human Fulfilment Needs is being met in your life.

Need	How are you meeting this need?	What more can you do?
Safety		
Connection		
Code		
Identity		
Competence		
Impact		
Freedom		

Human Fulfilment Wants

Once our Human Fulfilment Needs are being met, we want for other things: things that make us feel good about ourselves and about life in general. These are the Human Fulfilment Wants: things that add sparkle and give meaning to our lives.

When you can find avenues to express Human Fulfilment Wants, life is good. You are happy with your lot. You plod along and deal with the good and the bad in equal measure. You take things in your stride and, overall, you are happy. You can spend time with people who understand you and accept you for who you are. There are no apologies or modifications needed: these are your kind of people. All is well in your world... Well, that might be a bit of a stretch. Life is not *always* wonderful, but overall you get to do what you want. You get to go where you want. You have some plans for your life and even if things get tough at times, at least once a week you get that Friday feeling! You have the time, opportunity and resources to let your hair down and have some fun. (In my case, letting my hair down is purely metaphorical: my forehead has been elongating for quite some time now, so I don't have that luxury)

There are four Human Fulfilment Wants: empathy, pleasure, creative expression and goals.

Empathy

It feels really good to know that you are on the same wavelength as someone else and that you can be there for them in times of need or challenge. We love to give advice; it makes us feel important. We all seek to understand and to be understood. It gives us a sense of belonging and provides us with the ability to make meaningful connections. Empathy is the skill that allows us to form healthy relationships. It is the glue that bonds us together. It gives us the ability to walk a mile in another person's shoes. (And, as the joke says, if by that time you still don't understand them, at least you have their shoes and you're a mile away!)

Pleasure

Life is meant to be good. You are meant to enjoy it. You are meant to have fun. This does not have to be 'the valley of tears'. That is just someone else's take on it and they are well dead by now. As the saying goes: 'We are here for a good time, not for a long time!' I am Irish – the Roman Catholic variety. I always felt that Protestants were brought up to work hard but still enjoy life, while Roman Catholics were told to go forth and multiply but always remember that we were broken before we ever got started in life. But I didn't like fourth place: I'd prefer to come first. So, when I finished school, I finished with religion. I put pleasure on the table and guilt out the back door and things began to look up. It's not just girls that want to have fun: we all do! We all love to feel good, to be amused and entertained and to have intimacy in our lives. These are the good things in life. When they're kept in check, they make for the good times; let them get out of balance and they produce addiction, which diminishes our life experience. Just as *identity* underpins all of our Human Fulfilment Needs, our pursuit of *pleasure* underpins all of our Human Fulfilment Wants. How we pursue pleasure will determine the quality of experience that we glean from all of our Human Fulfilment Wants.

Creative Expression

The desire to express ourselves can be played out in many different ways. It can be as sophisticated as Beethoven's Symphony No. 5, as determined as Michelangelo's painting of the Sistine Chapel ceiling, or as rewarding as landscaping your own back garden. Whatever the end result, the desire is always the same. Each of us likes to invent, build, design or compose things. Human beings are inherently creative and when afforded the opportunity will express that. The guy that is unemployed for years may spend his days doing wonderful DIY projects at home. The stay-at-home mum may experiment with food, coming up with new recipes and combinations every day. The teenager who stays in his room may be writing music for his newly-formed band. Whatever situations humans are in, they will seek expression of some sort. In the absence of self-expression they get bored, frustrated and stunted; and many turn to food, drink or entertainment in order to fill the void.

Goals

As much as we need to express ourselves verbally, emotionally and practically, we also need a *structure* that will give us a sense of completion or finality. We need something to punctuate our experiences and give us a sense of control over our environment. Things need to happen in stages. Things need to have a beginning and an end; otherwise we get overwhelmed and lose interest. Apart from being vehicles for self-expression, goals give us direction, certainty and focus. When you have goals, you feel you are on track. You are making progress and you are moving forward. Goals offer structure and structure feels real. When you have structure, you feel in control. Without structure, we can feel listless, distracted, bored, irritable, uneasy and empty.

Summary

It is worth emphasising that the Human Fulfilment Wants are *wants* and not needs. We want them, we chase them, we look for them, but we do survive without them. The fulfilment of these desires certainly makes for a richer life. However, many people have lives that are less than desirable and this is because human beings are rarely taught how to live. They are expected to find out for themselves. Some people gain life experience from their parents, peers or culture; but obviously there are as many ways to live as there are neighbourhoods. Many people figure out the best way to live their lives, but many people do not. In fact, some are way off the mark. This is a chronic failure of society but, of course, it can be changed.

Exercise: Assessment of Human Fulfilment Wants

Assess how each of the Human Fulfilment Wants is being met in your life.

Want	How are you meeting this want?	What more can you do?
Empathy		
Pleasure		
Creative Expression		
Goals		

Human Fulfilment Possibilities

I have often heard someone respond to the question 'Are you happy?' with something like 'Yes, I am happy. Sure I have all that I need and I don't want for anything. What more could you ask for?' To be in a position to say this is indeed a great thing. It is something for which anyone would be eternally grateful.

When you examine the statement though, you will think of people who have all they could want but somehow are still not happy. I have some old school friends who appear to me to be frozen in time but they tell me they are happy. I know my path is not theirs and I respect that. Of course it is possible to be happy with your lot and more power to you if you are, but it is my opinion that it is in our nature to be always somewhat uncomfortable with some of the things in our life. It is not a bad thing to have an underlying tension that seeks release through expression. I believe this ensures our continual growth and evolution. In fact, the more uncomfortable you become with the way things are, the further you are inclined to reach deep down inside and come up with new things. The deeper you dig, the further you can go. The further you go, the more impact you can have on your own life and beyond. The possibilities are endless.

There are four Human Fulfilment Possibilities: growth, contribution, peak performance and transcendence.

Growth

You may have heard the saying that the only constant thing is change. Life is changing all the time and if we fail to change with it we get left behind. As much as we like to create things, we also like to learn things. It makes us feel like we are making progress. Haven't you noticed how you seem to come alive when you enter into the learning process? When new worlds are opened up to you and you see things with a fresh perspective, you gain a sense of power and control over your life.

Of course, we can choose to learn or not learn. How many times have you heard people say things like 'I am too old' or 'You can't teach an old dog new tricks'. One thing that is sure to accelerate old age is the unwillingness to learn new things. When a person stops learning, they stop growing. In my opinion, when a person stops growing mentally, they start to die.

Contribution

I believe that everything you have comes from energy and that energy was given to you. Whether it is a house, a friend or a thought, it all springs from the same source. You get to shape, mould and redefine it but it is not yours to keep; you just get to be in charge of it for now. This energy is what makes us one. So to give is really giving back to yourself.

It comes down to personal choice, of course. You can decide that what's yours is yours. You can decide that you have earned it and worked hard enough for it and you are not going to share it. But giving is an act that returns itself doublefold. The choice to help, assist or offer your time and attention to others raises your consciousness to a much higher level and gives you back so much more in return. The opportunity to improve the lives of others brings its own reward. Erich Fromm puts it so well:

> Giving is the highest expression of potency. In the very act of giving, I experience my strength, my wealth, my power. This experience of heightened vitality and potency fills me with joy. I experience myself as overflowing, spending, alive, hence as joyous. Giving is more joyous than receiving, not because it is a deprivation, but because in the act of giving lies the expression of my aliveness.

Peak Performance

Self-actualization is about reaching your full potential. When Abraham Maslow studied exemplary people such as Albert Einstein, Jane Addams, Eleanor Roosevelt and Frederick Douglass, he identified what he called a 'need' for self-actualization. According to Maslow, 'What a man can be, he must be.' Maslow spoke of people's desire to reach their full potential. It is my opinion that this is not a need but rather a *choice*. If it was a need, more people would be doing it. Maslow recognised that this 'being need' may differ from person to person. For example, one person may want to become an ideal parent, another may want to be the greatest artist, another the best musician, etc. So reaching your full potential involves choice. How exactly you choose to excel is up to you.

Transcendence

Transcendence is about exceeding your potential. Maslow referred to this as a tendency 'to become more and more what one is, to become everything that one is capable of becoming'. It is my belief that by becoming all that you can be you actually transcend what you originally were. Think about it: when you mix flour, sugar, butter, eggs and vanilla and place them in a cake tin in the oven, you know that the sum of these parts is going to amount to something different. The sponge cake is something entirely new that transcends the ingredients used.

Transcendence is a process that can only happen if you work to reach your full potential. The fact that we are called human beings shows that we are already engaged in a continuous process: the process of being. In nature, nothing stands still: everything is either growing, maturing, ripening or dying. As the Buddhists say, 'Everything is transient.' In this world, everything has a beginning and an end. Human beings are the species with the most choice and influence on this process. We do not get to choose the final outcome but we can influence the rate of its execution. You can decide whether to expand your mind or enrich your experience. You can decide to delve into the unknown. You can decide to stay as you are or to push the envelope. You can decide to gain more insight, knowledge, life experience and wisdom. More than this, you can decide to add your bit to the quantum soup. You can make a real contribution. Einstein did, Mozart did, Edison did, Martin Luther King did, Charlie Chaplin did, Jimi Hendrix did; and so can you.

Exercise: Assessment of Human Fulfilment Possibilities

Assess each of the Human Fulfilment Possibilities in your life.

Possibility	What are you doing now to make this happen?	What can help you to improve?
Growth		Study the art and science of success.
Contribution		Share your knowledge.
Peak performance		Output your skills frequently.
Transcendence		Stick with it – you can do it!

Human Fulfilment Distractions

In life, knowing what to do and how to do it is never enough. You need to create the time, put in the effort, avoid the distractions and remove the obstacles. Then and only then are you on your way to success.

There are four key Human Fulfilment Distractions: pleasure, denial, withdrawal and blame.

Pleasure

If you are lucky enough to be able to meet your survival and other basic needs, then your quality of life will be determined by how you manage your pleasure pursuits. The pursuit of pleasure is a double-edged sword. It can be an *attraction* and a *distraction* at the same time.

The Measure of Pleasure

We continuously chase pleasure but it operates best on the principle of moderation. An over-indulgence of any particular pleasure can produce an addiction, so the best approach is to have a little of what you like – and often. In saying this, I am not trying to be a killjoy: pleasure has many dimensions to it. It is when we narrow our focus onto one strand of it that an imbalance occurs and this leads to problems. To get the most out of life, you need to widen your experiences of pleasure. In that way, you actually get to experience a lot more pleasure overall.

Pleasure works on two levels. The first level is instant gratification. Food provides us with this sort of pleasure: we smell it, taste it, eat it and instantly feel good. The next level of pleasure requires a build-up of tension, followed by its release. This is the pleasure that comes from achieving a goal or challenge, or taking part in an event you've been looking forward to. This form of pleasure generally requires effort in advance; and the greater our effort, the greater our expectation. 'If I work really hard I will succeed; if I stick with the diet I will lose weight; if I endure the pain of the gym I will look great on the beach.' You know the drill.

What this teaches us is that pleasure is not constant. It cannot be. It is an emotion; and emotions by their nature are *in motion*. They travel through peaks and troughs. They have thresholds that, when reached, are followed by a natural decline. Some are paced differently but all of them take the same path. A man can be happy doing the same job for twenty years and gradually become fed up of it, lose interest and seek something else. The addict can get a huge kick from the first few hits and then find that he is forever chasing this same high, but all it does is maintain a level of perceived normality. The adrenaline-seeker is always chasing the bigger thrill. It is in the nature of pleasure that we always seek more of it. Religion is never the opium of the people; pleasure is.

The Science of Pleasure

Recent research suggests that there is a 'pleasure principle' at the heart of human decision-making. The experience of pleasure comes about by the release of the neurotransmitter dopamine into our system. This is what produces the feel-good effect and makes us seek more pleasure. So, you now have a good excuse if someone gives you a hard time for over-indulging. Tell them it wasn't your fault: the dopamine made you do it!

The SEAL model of Subjective Pleasure

The reasons why we seek pleasure can be summed up by the SEAL model: sensory stimulation, entertainment, accomplishment and love.

- *Sensory Stimulation:* We all love the things that excite our senses: the flavour of food, a kiss on the lips, the comfort of a hot bath, the feeling of a summer breeze on our skin. Our senses are designed to delight in these.
- *Entertainment:* We all love to have fun, laugh and have our curiosity aroused. No matter what age we are, we all love to play games, have parties and daydream.
- *Accomplishment:* We love when we invent, build, design, work, compose, achieve and produce new things. We love when we get recognition, respect, admiration and approval for our efforts. We enjoy surrounding ourselves with possessions that symbolise our achievements.
- *Love:* We love our relationships, friendships and families – maybe not all the time, but overall we do! We love to share, take care of people, make love and express our emotions and ideas. We love privacy and intimate spaces of togetherness.

The Pleasure Cycle

For human beings, the pleasure button is forever on the 'seek' position. We are always either indulging in pleasure or looking for it. When we get pleasure, we indulge in it and then move on to seeking more.

It unfolds something like this:

> I feel hungry. *(Pleasure is absent.)*
> I think I'd like something nice to eat. *(Seek mode.)*
> I sit down to have my meal. *(Pleasure mode.)*
> I eat my food. *(Indulgent mode.)*
> I eat too much. *(Pleasure is absent again.)*
> I think it'd be good to walk it off. *(Seek mode again.)*
> I walk. *(Shift towards pleasure mode.)*
> My body feels refreshed. *(Pleasure mode again.)*

A healthy pleasure cycle operates in this way:

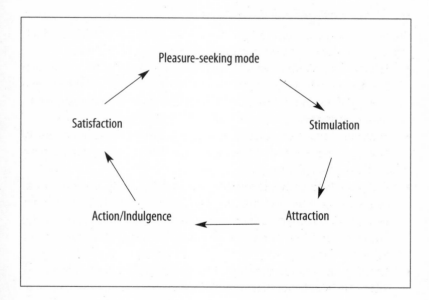

The Pleasure Cycle of Over-Indulgence

Pleasure cycles do not always operate in the healthy way shown above. When you place too much emphasis on a particular pleasure, you get addicted and this throws your life out of balance. It steals your time, occupies your mind and lowers your mood. The pleasure gained at the start is increasingly reduced, while the tension connected to it grows all the time. This is a lose-lose situation. Distraction can provide the solution, but the distraction needs to have a focus and be able to replace the previous pleasure with a new one.

An unhealthy pleasure cycle can unfold in this way:

> I feel hungry. *(Pleasure is absent.)*
> I think I'd like something nice to eat. *(Seek mode.)*
> I sit down to have my meal. *(Pleasure mode.)*
> I eat my food. *(Indulgent mode.)*
> I eat too much. *(Pleasure is absent again.)*
> I think it'd be good to walk it off. *(Seek mode again.)*
> I decide it's not worth the effort. *(Still in seek mode.)*
> I sit at the table a while longer. *(Still in seek mode.)*
> I know I have had enough but the food looks tempting. *(Still in seek mode.)*
> I start to nibble and pick. *(Pleasure mode.)*
> I know I am stuffed but it tastes so nice. *(I feel conflicted.)*
> I eat some more and begin to feel bloated. *(I feel guilty.)*
> I am too stuffed to move. *(I feel more conflicted.)*
> I do nothing. *(I feel empty.)*
> I sit. *(I feel bored.)*
> I continue to sit. *(I feel anxious.)*
> I think I'd better do something. *(I begin to get distracted.)*
> A neighbour calls in. *(I am distracted.)*
> I offer them tea. *(I am distracted.)*
> I put biscuits on the table. *(I am tempted.)*
> I look at the biscuits as we chat. *(I am stimulated.)*
> I reach for a biscuit. *(Pleasure mode.)*

These unhealthy pleasure cycles lead to over-indulgence and addiction.

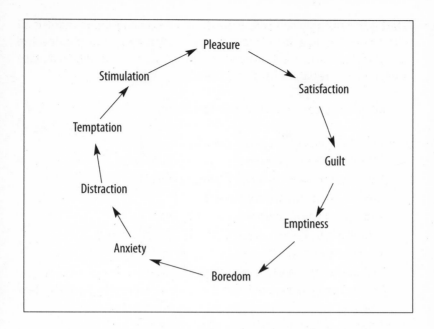

Recovery Mindset in Seven Steps

The seven steps below can help you to deal with over-indulgence of a particular pleasure.

1. Acknowledge that the reason you are doing this is that it feels good. Be okay with that. You are simply doing what everyone on the planet wants to do, which is to enjoy yourself.

2. Now move your thinking to the long-term consequences of continuing to behave in this way. Remind yourself how the behaviour makes you feel. Think about how you would like to feel instead. It is important to avoid any negative internal commentary. Take this as a project and apply your logical mind to it. You are creating an exit strategy from one behaviour and an entry point for a new behaviour.

3. Set aside your opinion on the behaviour and track what you want in the long-term. Assume the role of a scientist and go into clinical observation mode. When the opportunity for pleasure arises, be aware of it. Notice how you respond to it. Check in with it. Mark out the steps involved. Slow everything down, including your behaviour. Track it step by step. Forget about what you already know and try to view everything with fresh eyes.

4. Sort through your feelings as they arise. Question them. Is this a good feeling or a bad one? Is this a clouded feeling or a natural one? In the moment, ask yourself what it is that you want. Do not try to reject the pleasure or to distract yourself from it. Be with it, stay with it, and now begin to add to it.
5. Introduce your commentary. Remind yourself what it is that you want. Use the Pleasure Before Pressure technique (see below). Stay with the experience; remain there as you experience the unveiling of the new behaviour.
6. It makes no difference whether you succeed completely or partially. Everything you have done has altered your pattern. Think long-term, if needed.
7. Every time you are faced with the challenge of over-indulgence or addiction, resume your practice. You can be certain that, in time, you will succeed. No matter what happens, refuse negative commentary. You are in skill-building mode.

The Pleasure Before Pressure Technique

You know ahead of time that temptation will rise, so get ready for it! Grab a moment or two for some uninterrupted thinking. Spend time inside your mind, visualising how you will look, feel and behave differently when you are free from the attraction to your particular pleasure.

Create a mental movie of yourself. Visualise various situations where previously you would have been tempted, but you are now happy, relaxed, enthusiastic and free. Add dialogue to your movie. Be positive: speak to yourself, support yourself, praise yourself and encourage yourself. Speak about the future benefits of different behaviour and the greater pleasure of long-term success. In your movie, imagine yourself stressed, tired, frustrated or overwhelmed. Visualise being able to overcome these feelings. See the dullness of struggle and exasperation give way to powerful feelings of freedom. As you visualise these events, breathe in deeply and soak up the lighter, brighter, happier, successful feelings!

Take the view that each time you are faced with a challenge, you are also just seconds away from yet another breakthrough. Focus on the delicious *feeling* that goes with success. Amp up that feeling, run it through your mind many, many times. Whenever you have a free moment, recall that feeling. Collect the heightened pleasure that goes with it. Let it bathe all the cells of your being. Remember that every time you are challenged, it is another opportunity to improve, enjoy more freedom and become the master of your own destiny.

Denial
There are times that we will do anything but the task at hand. We will dodder, dither, doodle, muck about, waste time, lay about – anything rather than do what we are supposed to do. This is all about the Law of Tension. All goals produce a level of tension and, because we are pleasure-seekers, we often try to avoid the tension by denying ourselves in order to keep us from doing what we really need to be doing. Denial comes in different forms, e.g. we draw on fantasy by pushing our hope into things that we really don't believe in. I have seen this many times in my line of work. People build a fantasy and fall in love with the idea of it, all the while ignoring reality. Denial is futile: all it does is produce more tension. The solution to denial is appropriate action.

Withdrawal
At times, we are all guilty of pulling back from life and giving into whatever is easiest. We can take the lazy way out and simply allow life to happen to us, rather than actively pursuing our dreams and ambitions. Some people pull back from life before they ever even take a step forward. These people spend their lives in supporting roles, allowing *other* people to achieve *their* hopes and dreams, all the while withdrawing from the pursuit of any aspirations of their own. This behaviour can lead to lethargy, depression, bitterness and even sickness. Human beings do not get away with withdrawal. We are designed to be self-expressive and any thwarting of that need leads to a twisting of the psyche.

Blame
Blame is a favourite, especially for many Irish people. I, for one, am guilty of it at times. Many Irish people blamed the British for a lot of things and then, when Queen Elizabeth II visited and spoke to us in Irish, they shifted their blame for current circumstances onto the Germans! Now, before anyone takes up arms, it has to be said that circumstances can be complex and blame is sometimes well-earned. However, this is not always the case. When we blame, we actually let ourselves off the hook. When we criticise – which is just the other side of the same coin – we put ourselves

on a pedestal. *We* know better. I've always liked the saying: 'If you have nothing good to say, then say nothing at all.' (Although, I'll admit that if I was to live by it, I'd be quiet an awful lot of the time …) Blaming is easy to do but let's face it, most blaming is actually failing: failing to be responsible, failing to step up and be accountable for your own life.

Exercise: Assessment of Human Fulfilment Distractions

Assess each of the Human Fulfilment Distractions in your life.

Distractions	What are your distractions?	How can you fix them?
Pleasure		
Denial		
Withdrawal		
Blame		

Human Fulfilment Obstacles

Distractions are actions and behaviours that we put in place in order to mask our underlying goals and objectives. In addition to these, there are four Human Fulfilment Obstacles: fear, uncertainty, challenge and resistance.

Fear

Fear is sometimes used as an excuse but it is not without solid foundation. Sometimes we are *afraid* of the consequences of fulfilment. Most people claim they would like to be successful, but many people actually have a fear of it. This is evident in the self-sabotaging behaviours of many celebrities.

Uncertainty

For the most part, we don't do so well with too much uncertainty. I had a conversation with a client recently who had concerns about making the decision to settle down, get married and start a family. Thoughts whirled around his mind as he wondered what would happen in the future. Would he make a good dad? Did he really want to be a dad? Should he get married? Would it suit him? What if it didn't work out? What would he have to give up? Would he be throwing away an old way of life that he was actually really happy with?

Uncertainty rarely comes without fear, and this particular client had the two going on full blast. We spoke for a while and I explained that, while there are no guarantees in life, there are always choices. We always have the opportunity to change paths or to improve the path we have chosen. This client's path couldn't be worked out fully ahead of time: there were too many variables. However, in the face of uncertainty, one thing he certainly could commit to is *flexibility*. If he got married and it didn't work out, he could always get a divorce. If he had children and didn't know how to parent them, he could always get help with that.

I reminded my client that the very fact that he was giving such serious consideration to marriage before making a commitment meant that he was likely to treat it with value, which is a great place to start. My client loves his partner, he's a downright decent bloke and I've every faith that he would make a great dad; but this is a path that he needs to walk down himself in order to fully find out. His decision will definitely be coloured by this process and by thinking through what life would be like if he chose *not* to go down that path. In NLP we call this an Ecological Check.

Challenge

Goals produce tension but if the goal is too big (or it just feels that way) we are likely to hold back. This is a double-edged sword: the greater the challenge, the greater the benefit. That is why it is so important to focus more on where you want to go than where you are at any given time.

Resistance

If you are resisting something, you need to discover what it is that is holding you back. Resistance comes from internal conflict. It could be a belief or value; if it is, no amount of effort will overcome it. Resistance causes unnecessary and unhealthy tension. Fortunately, we have ways and means of dealing with it. These will be explored later on in the section on beliefs (see Chapter 8).

Exercise: Assessment of Human Fulfilment Obstacles

Assess each of the Human Fulfilment Obstacles in your life.

Obstacles	What obstacles do you face?	How can you overcome them?
	Fear	
Uncertainty		
Challenge		
Resistance		

Now that you have made an assessment of where *you* are, read Chapter 2 for some lessons from people who made it to where *they* wanted to be.

Lessons from the Extraordinary

What the caterpillar calls the end of the world,
the Master calls a butterfly.

Richard Bach

Albert Einstein was no good at remembering birthdays and everyday events. He stopped wearing socks from a young age after discovering that his big toes always ended up making a hole in them. Bruce Lee was short-sighted and, on numerous occasions, nearly got killed crossing the road. He never had any formal qualifications in martial arts and he was a great fan of the footwork of Muhammad Ali. In fact, he spoke of wanting to become a boxer so that he could fight him one day. Ali himself is famous for his objection to the Vietnam War but many people forget that he actually failed the initial qualifying test for the military because his spelling and writing were deemed to be under-par. It's hard to imagine that a man of his intellect would ever be viewed in that way. Leonardo da Vinci had seventeen siblings, was vegetarian and didn't go to school much. He had a love for birds and animals and used to buy them in the markets so that he could set them free. Charlie Chaplin once won third prize in a Charlie Chaplin lookalike contest. He must have felt out of sorts that day! Thomas Edison was practically deaf and it seems he liked it that way, as it allowed him to concentrate better on his work. Sir Isaac Newton wasn't hit on the head with an apple. He was actually looking out of his bedroom window when he saw the apple fall from the tree and that's how he came up with his theory of gravity.

Plenty of folklore surrounds these people. Each was an individual with quirks, circumstances and personality traits all their own. They had their idiosyncrasies but they were also 'normal' in their own ways. They certainly had moments of glory, but they weren't busy being extraordinary every single moment of their lives. In this chapter, I want to explore the worlds of some of these people. They came from many different fields and they were unique in many ways, but when we examine their lives, patterns emerge that are common to all of them.

While these people were geniuses in many ways, this chapter is not an examination of genius. It is more about learning from people with extraordinary and exceptional lives. We will examine the tools, techniques and strategies of these people, as well as their attitudes to success and their setbacks. This, coupled with NLP, will allow you to create a model of excellence for yourself. What you learn in this chapter is just the beginning, though. As you proceed, each chapter will reveal to you something more that you can do to further your progress.

The Genius of Albert Einstein

One of the best-known and most documented minds of all time is that of the father of modern-day physics, Albert Einstein. Few people haven't heard of the $E = mc^2$ Theory of Relativity or seen his face and wild-looking haircut in a book or online. As a result of his incredible intelligence and originality, his name will forever be associated with the word 'genius'. So what advice can a genius like Einstein teach you about living an exceptional life?

Think for Yourself and Question Everything

We live in a world full of expertise, with people constantly shoving their own ideas and life perspectives down our throats. Fortunately – and particularly with the advent of the internet – few statements go unchallenged. There will always be a sceptical and sometimes cynical mind that will question the validity of any claim.

Einstein himself was not afraid to think independently and challenge the norm. Even as a teenager, he challenged his teachers with the idea that critical thinking was far more important for learning than simple rote learning or memorisation. The key to critical thinking is to question assumptions. It has its foundations in the Socratic Method, developed by the philosopher Socrates. He promoted debate among his students as a way of teaching and as a way of developing independent thinking. It makes sense to question something before you take it on board as fact or belief. The infamous Harvard professor Timothy Leary is known for saying, 'Think for yourself and question authority.' Richard Bandler, one of the original co-developers of NLP, has said, 'Never trust a theory.' After all, a theory is just someone else's world view. A good friend of mine who was reared on the Falls Road in Belfast during the Troubles told me that her dad, an educated man, always taught her to question things. So whenever a report appeared on the news or an article appeared in the newspaper, he would tell her to ask two basic questions: *Who says?* and *Why now?*

In Chapter 8, we will take this approach to a much deeper level and you will learn about the value of questioning and how to do it with greater ease and precision.

Lighten Up

Brilliance and misery are not necessary bedfellows. Einstein became so famous that he was recognisable on the streets of America, but when people approached him, he would claim he wasn't himself – just for the fun of it. A quick search online will show you many photos of him pulling silly faces for the camera – this is the stuff of genius! Thanks to scientific research, we now know that you are smarter when you are smiling than when you are frowning. So, in order to keep your brain fit you should have more fun. Personally, I can't see why anyone could take this life seriously. There is no point: you are never going to get out alive anyway, so you might as well enjoy yourself in the meantime!

Master Your Mood — and Stick With It

Einstein produced over 300 scientific research papers and 150 non-scientific works. He did this through perspiration, not inspiration alone. Einstein was focused and had a dogged determination. He once explained that most people who were asked to find a needle in a haystack would stop when they found it. He said that would not satisfy him, though. He would continue to look for more, just to ensure that he had captured all of the possibilities. This type of dedication requires self-discipline. You can be sure there were days Einstein didn't want to go to work, but he overcame his mood and got on with the job at hand. Mood is not a good guide for behaviour, as mood can be triggered by so many variables. If you want to become better, there will be times when you need to focus on the bigger picture, set aside your duller moments and simply put your nose to the grindstone.

There is No Such Thing as Failure, Unless You Have Given Up

Einstein was okay with not getting it right all of the time. This is a core principle in NLP: 'There is no such thing as failure, only feedback.' Einstein considered 'getting it wrong' as simply a part of the process on the way to getting it right. So if he got it wrong, he used the information gained from this experience and moved on. He also believed that if you get criticised, you gather the information from the criticism and determine whether it contains anything useful to help you move closer to your goal. Remember, the reason some criticism hurts is because it may have an element of truth in it. It's best to disregard the *way* in which criticism is delivered (usually badly), but take the message contained within the criticism, use it and move forward with it. Your critics can go to extremes to find fault in your ideas. You can use this constructively to think in ways you wouldn't have originally. Of course, some criticism is just meanness, so you need realise that and treat it appropriately. And it's important to create your *own* definition of success. Einstein had this to say, 'Try not to be become a man of success, but rather a man of value.'

Exercise: Image-Streaming

Creativity expert Win Wenger invented a process called 'image-streaming', which stimulates your brain and promotes creativity. Try it and you'll be as smart as Einstein in no time!

1. Sit in front of your video recorder or computer and begin to record a video of yourself.
2. Close your eyes.
3. Take a moment to relax.
4. Now bring your attention to the stream of thoughts entering your mind.
5. Describe aloud what you perceive, hear, feel, smell and taste. Do this instantly, as the thoughts surface.
6. Continue this for 5–15 minutes.
7. When you are finished, play back what you have recorded.

If you like, you could do this with a partner so that you can discuss your experience afterwards.

The Creativity of Leonardo da Vinci

Artist, architect, inventor and scientist – Leonardo da Vinci had one of the most creative minds of all time. He also stands out as one of the best-rounded individuals and a lot can be learned from his approach to life.

Search for Patterns in Apparently Unrelated Things

In his relentless pursuit of excellence, Leonardo da Vinci did not discriminate. He had an insatiable curiosity and saw all knowledge as being valuable and connected. Knowledge in one area always offers insight into another and da Vinci's wide range of skills proves this fact. He was constantly looking for connections and in so doing came up with so many life-altering concepts.

Write Everything Down

Da Vinci placed huge value on getting his thoughts and ideas on paper as soon as they came to him. Writing down your ideas as soon as they come does two things: it lets your brain know that the idea is of value; and it frees up your mind to expand on the idea subconsciously. How many times have you had an idea that slipped away from you because you were too distracted to write it down?

Exercise: Invest in a Portable Memory Bank

Win Wenger recommends the use of what he calls a 'portable memory bank'. By this he means a pocket-sized notebook that you take with you wherever you go so that you can capture your ideas and observations. This may appear a little old-fashioned in a digital age, and you could use a smart phone instead, but the exercise of physically writing down an idea tends to engage more of your attention. Whatever method you choose, the key thing is to start recording and then review the material on a regular basis.

Keep on Learning

Da Vinci believed that, in order to maximise your full potential, you should commit to four principles: study art; study science; learn how to develop all your senses, especially visual; and study with the view that all of these things are connected. Fortunately, the brain is a pattern-making machine, so this process of connection tends to happen automatically. However, it makes sense to be aware and deliberate in your approach. Richard Bandler once gave similar advice to my business partner when he said: 'You should do as many different things and go to as many different places as possible, and you should learn as many things from as many different people as possible.'

The Business Skills of Thomas Edison

Thomas Edison, controversial American creator and businessman, is credited with the invention of many things, including the light bulb. One of the most prolific inventors of all time, he had 1,093 patents to his name. Learning about his approach to life can inspire us to improve our own.

Keep it Current

Edison was hugely practical and realistic. He was well aware of the fact that an idea too far ahead of its time was less likely to succeed than one that was on trend, so he paced his progress accordingly.

If You Can't Innovate, Immovate

One of Edison's most famous quotes is: 'Genius is one per cent inspiration, ninety-nine per cent perspiration.' Edison himself did not rely on inspiration and perspiration alone to come up with ideas and inventions. He always watched to see what other inventors were up to. He then took these ideas and either came up with the invention that was not yet created, or he expanded on the latest invention and made it even better. This concept of expanding and improving on an idea is now known as 'immovation'. The strength of the Chinese economy is based on this. Knowing that creativity is not necessarily their best asset, the Chinese have focused on *immovation* and have become masters of this form of enterprise. Of course, *innovation* is still vital for every new generation. Apple is a company that shows great innovation and they add a good dash of creativity and marketing into the mix when coming up with products that people love to buy.

Create a Mastermind Group

In addition to studying other inventors, Edison surrounded himself with like-minded people so that he could stoke the creative fires. He realised that two minds are better than one, so he created his own invention factory. In his factory, he gathered the great young minds of the time (including people like Nikola Tesla) and tapped into their talents and abilities.

Exercise: Create Your Mastermind Group

Mastermind Group Member	What can they bring to the table?

You Have to Sell Your Ideas

Edison knew that no matter how timely an idea was, it still needed a helping hand. He recognised the value of *persuasion* in the selling of an idea. He displayed great passion in talking about his inventions and he went to great lengths to demonstrate them in the most exciting, impressive and memorable ways. Take a look at some Apple advertisements and you will see that a lot of effort goes into *selling the concept* – and it works. Steve Jobs was a master of this form of persuasion.

Put Your Ideas to the Test — Repeatedly

Ever the pragmatist, Edison recognised the value of feedback. He tested and re-tested his ideas, constantly modifying them until he was confident that they worked. This practice of testing brings an idea into the material world, which is where it will ultimately succeed or fail. Many of us have ideas but, until we do something about them, that's all they are. They mean nothing until they are tried and tested in the real world.

You Have to Put in the Work

Edison held himself to very demanding standards and insisted on an 'idea quota'. This quota required that he come up with a minor invention every ten days and a major invention every six months. He may not always have achieved this quota; but just having it meant he achieved far more overall. If you want to get things done, your brain needs a target. When it comes to productivity and output, your brain does not do well with open-ended projects; you are likely to wander and get distracted.

Boost Your Energy and Creativity by Power Napping

Edison was known to lie down on his workbench and take a twenty-minute rest break, which he called his 'power nap'. During this time, he could recharge and he also had flashes of inspiration and often came up with new ideas. The states of mind he entered were what we now refer to as *alpha state* and *theta state*. These are altered states of consciousness, which can be induced more quickly through relaxation meditation and hypnosis. Using the CD that accompanies this book, *Mind of Genius*, will help you to enter into these creative mind states.

The Flexibility of Bruce Lee

Bruce Lee was an actor, film director and philosopher. He founded Jeet Kune Do, a hybrid martial arts system of combat. Lee is considered to be the most influential martial artist of the twentieth-century, as well as a pop culture icon. His approach to martial arts was quite philosophical and inspiring.

Apply What You Learn

Lee believed that success was not governed by the accumulation of knowledge but by the practical application of that knowledge. There is a time for learning and a time for doing. You must output what you input; otherwise you stay put!

There is Elegance in Simplicity

Lee was not slavish to tradition. He approached his craft from all directions and stripped it back to bare essentials, sorting all the time for effectiveness and removing anything that was not needed. In this way, he removed the mysterious rituals and ceremonies associated with the martial arts disciplines of his time. By combining knowledge from many sources and distilling it into its simplest form, he created something entirely new.

Learn the Rules, then Let Them Go

Lee was a firm believer in discipline. He once said that he would not fear the man who has practised 10,000 kicks once, but he would fear the man who has practised one kick 10,000 times. He recognised the value of disciplined effort as the foundation for skill development. Equally, he felt that once a skill was mastered, it should be let go. There should be a trust that the movement will come to you when you most need it. This ties in with Abraham Maslow's principle of *detachment*.

Be Flexible

Lee believed that in life, just as in combat, there comes a time when the plan becomes obsolete. You have to be prepared to change and adapt in order to stay ahead of the game; otherwise you are in danger of getting left behind.

There are No Limits

Lee always advocated pushing past your perceived limits. According to him, there are no limits, only *plateaus*. If you find yourself at a plateau, you must not stay there; you must push past it. He once said, 'Awareness has no frontier; it is giving of your whole being, without exclusion.'

Exercise: Push Through Your Plateaus		
Your plateaus	Five reasons for each. Why are you stuck?	Describe what it would feel like to push past each reason.

The Empathy of Oprah Winfrey

Oprah Winfrey is a talk show host, actress and producer. She is considered to be one of the most influential women in the world today and she ranks as one of the greatest philanthropists. Her talk show ran for twenty-five years and was the highest-rated in history; it is thought to have popularised and revolutionised the genre.

Educate Yourself

Born into poverty, Oprah experienced considerable hardship during her childhood. She is a survivor of sexual abuse. First raped at age nine, she became pregnant at fourteen and her son died shortly after birth. Despite all of this, she decided to take responsibility for herself and to work hard to overcome her situation. She knew that education was vital and she read voraciously. Books gave her hope and taught her that if others could overcome tough circumstances, so could she.

Be True to Yourself

Oprah believes that you should not let others tell you what can and can't do. You cannot live your life to please others. You must take responsibility for your own life and you must live it with passion!

Be the Best You Can Be

Oprah is living proof that if you do the best you can do, and be the best you can be, you will have everything you need in life. Strive for something better. Surround yourself with people that are as smart as you are – or even smarter! Work on getting rid of any addictions, whether they are to food, alcohol or drugs. Remain patient until you get there.

Find the Opportunity in the Challenge

Oprah uses her own life experiences for the greater good, for empathy and compassion. She allows herself to be open, honest and vulnerable in order to effect change. By being authentic, she created powerful and meaningful connections and rose to the level of influence and success she holds today.

Exercise: Scamper Technique

Think of an issue that is getting in the way of your success and use the SCAMPER technique to come up with solutions. Can you:

Substitute something?

Combine it with something else?

Adapt something?

Modify or change it in some way?

Put it to some other use?

Eliminate something?

Rearrange or reverse it?

The Self-Love of Charlie Chaplin

Sir Charles Spencer, best known by his stage name Charlie Chaplin, was an English comic actor, film director and composer during the silent film era. With his unique blend of mime, slapstick and other visual comedy routines, he became the most famous film star in the world.

The following poem has been attributed to Charlie Chaplin. Some people say that he wrote it on the occasion of his seventieth birthday, but others dispute this fact. Whatever the poem's source, it captures Chaplin's attitude to life and, because of this, it will forever be associated with him.

As I Began to Love Myself

As I began to love myself I found that anguish and emotional suffering were only warning signs that I was living against my own truth.

Today, I know, this is **authenticity**.

As I began to love myself I understood how much it can offend somebody to force my desires on this person, even though I knew the time was not right and the person was not ready for it, and even though this person was me.

Today I call it **respect**.

As I began to love myself I stopped craving for a different life, and I could see that everything that surrounded me was inviting me to grow.

Today I call it **maturity**.

As I began to love myself I understood that at any circumstance, I am in the right place at the right time, and everything happens at the exactly right moment, so I could be calm.

Today I call it **self-confidence**.

As I began to love myself I quit stealing my own time, and I stopped designing huge projects for the future. Today, I only do what brings me joy and happiness, things I love to do and that make my heart cheer, and I do them in my own way and in my own rhythm.

Today I call it **simplicity**.

As I began to love myself I freed myself of anything that was no good for my health – food, people, things, situations, and everything that drew me down and away from myself. At first I called this attitude a healthy egoism.

Today I know it is **love of oneself**.

As I began to love myself I quit trying to always be right, and ever since, I was wrong less of the time.

Today I discovered that is **modesty**.

As I began to love myself I refused to go on living in the past and worrying about the future. Now, I only live for the moment, where **everything** is happening.

Today I live each day, day by day, and I call it **fulfilment**.

As I began to love myself I recognised that my mind can disturb me and it can make me sick. But as I connected it to my heart, my mind became a valuable ally.

Today I call this connection **wisdom of the heart**.

We no longer need to fear arguments, confrontations or any kind of problems with ourselves or others. Even stars collide, and out of their crashing, new worlds are born.

Today I know **that is life!**

By now you will see a pattern in the lives of all of the people featured in this chapter. They are different people who lived in different times and came from different walks of life, but they share common values and ideals. Psychologist Abraham Maslow was fascinated by these kinds of patterns in the lives of different people. He dedicated himself to the study of the positive qualities of exemplary people including: scientist Albert Einstein; philosopher, sociologist, author, women's suffrage and peace activist Jane Addams; civil rights activist Eleanor Roosevelt; and social reformer, orator, writer and statesman Frederick Douglass. Maslow later extended his research to include other people and this led to his Theory of Motivation.

I have incorporated Maslow's Theory of Motivation into the Wheel of Human Potential in Chapter 1. Maslow came up with the term 'self-actualization' and he used it to explain the process that must be undertaken by any individual if they are to reach their full potential. NLP, often described as the study of excellence, has examined Maslow's ideas and provides various models to discover exactly what it is that makes the difference between a person of ordinary skill and a person of exquisite skill.

Twenty-Four Things Valued by Extraordinary People

Independence

Extraordinary people walk to the beat of their own drum. They are self-directed and self-motivated. They will not let anyone tell them who they can or cannot be, what they can or cannot do. They like to be their own boss. They enjoy being self-sufficient, standing on their own two feet and making their own way in life.

Responsibility

Extraordinary people value their work. They take their responsibilities seriously and thrive on seeing them through. They do not fear them, hedge them or avoid them.

Logic

Extraordinary people are logical and shrewd. They are capable of using logic to be able to see both sides of the story before coming to a conclusion. They can accept that the world is the way it is and at the same time seek to improve it.

Perfection

Extraordinary people are driven towards perfection, continuously seeking to be the best they can be at what they do. They also appreciate the work and talents of others, if it meets these criteria. They feel that if a thing is worth doing it is worth doing correctly. Their version of right is perfection. They love to be in the company of other people who are exceptional at what they do.

Beauty

Extraordinary people value love, innocence, virtue, serenity and all things beautiful. They allow themselves to be affected, absorbed and immersed in it. They can fully appreciate and live in the moment.

Uniqueness

Extraordinary people love to be different and they love different things. They enjoy spontaneity and they love originality. This gives them their sense of individuality, which they are ferociously proud of and eager to declare given any opportunity.

Pragmatism

Extraordinary people like things that work; they enjoy making things that work. They determine things according to their usefulness and work to remove or improve things that don't work properly.

Challenge

Extraordinary people are energised by the presence of a challenge and will work relentlessly until they have mastered it. Any opportunity to make something better is a source for stimulation.

Creativity

Extraordinary people love being creative and using their imagination to come up with new ideas. They rely heavily on their intuition for guidance and it is this that makes them appear unconventional and 'off the wall' at times.

Improvement

Extraordinary people believe that anything that can be improved ought to be improved. They are always on the lookout for ways and ideas that can bring about improvement. They love anything that improves operations; anything that involves doing more with less or for less, without negatively impacting performance and quality.

Effortless Efficiency

Extraordinary people enjoy grace, elegance, efficiency, lack of strain and smoothness of progress. They have beautiful functionality and a waste-not-want-not attitude to the things they value.

Simplicity

Extraordinary people like to keep things simple. They want you to get to the point as quickly as possible. They love to get to the heart of the matter. They like to remove the illusion and get down to the facts.

Completion

Extraordinary people like things to be done. They are finishers. They cannot abide things being left half-done or undone; they view this as mediocrity. They don't like it in others and they refuse to accept it in themselves. They like to solve problems.

Richness

Extraordinary people appreciate richness. While they like things to be done as efficiently as possible, they also have an appreciation for depth and complexity. They feel that everything that needs to be included should be included. They like when nothing is hidden or missing. When they complete a process, everything is as it is and it needs no further alteration, modification, improvement or rearrangement. This is how masterpieces come about.

Mystery

Extraordinary people are attracted to making the unknown known. They want to solve the unsolvable and explain the inexplicable. Mystery doesn't faze them; it inspires them.

Playfulness

Extraordinary people usually have a great sense of humour are a little mischievous. They are playful and they like to enjoy things and be amused.

Spontaneity

Extraordinary people are not afraid of immediate action. While others are procrastinating, they are already doing. They like to hit the ground running and to clean up their mistakes as they go. The Wright brothers found out how to get their plane to fly through trial and error, while other scientists were busy in their laboratories working on theories.

Gratitude

Extraordinary people realise the power of gratitude. They value what they have and they are grateful for it.

Humility

Extraordinary people are humble. External flattery, social recognition, prestige or popularity does not do anything for them. They do not seek it because they do not value it.

Compassion

Extraordinary people do not do mean things and are incensed when others do. They like to give. They like to see others benefit and grow. They enjoy helping out and making people happy. They want the world to be a better place.

Family

Extraordinary people love their families and find it especially inspiring when children and young people grow and develop well. When my personal mentor Richard Bandler was asked what he considered to be the single most important thing in life, his answer was: 'Family ... family means everything.' When you have the backing of family, you can do almost anything. Extraordinary people *know* this. If their family of birth does not play a big part in their lives, they will ensure that they develop their own version of family by creating deep and long-lasting relationships with others of their choosing.

Social Duty

Extraordinary people believe that it is only right that the one who knows more should be tolerant, helpful and understanding to the one who might know less. They believe that every person should have the right to reach their full potential.

Justice

Extraordinary people have a deep desire to get to the truth and to fight for it. They often take up the cause of the underdog. They don't like to see people getting away with doing bad things and they delight in setting things right. They object to cruelty and any form of exploitation. They love happy endings and they like to see people being rewarded for their talents and the good things they do. They enjoy doing good things themselves and they generally choose a few of their own causes and make up their own minds about them, rather than being influenced by others.

Harmony

Extraordinary people like peace and calm. They are comfortable with being by themselves. They dislike turmoil, arguments and fighting. They can remove themselves from it and can enjoy themselves while everyone else gets bogged down.

How to Become More Extraordinary Than You Already Are

Decide Your Mission

Extraordinary people are planners: they have decided where their life is headed and they hold clear, compelling and precise inner pictures of what they want to accomplish. This ability is fundamental to your success, so throughout this book there will be plenty of guidance to help you on your way. If you don't have a life plan, you might find my first book, *The Happiness Habit*, helpful in creating one.

Choose Only the Goals That Excite You

No matter how well-meaning or noble your intentions may be, if your chosen goals fail to excite you, there is no way you will be able to remain focused in times of challenge or duress. Motivation is dependent on inspiration. If you want to live an exceptional life, you need to choose the goals that lift your heart and make your life worth living. The goals you choose need to be strong enough to pull you from tiredness, to lift you from laziness and to draw you away from passivity. In a nutshell, they need to light your fire! If your goal is well chosen, it will spark an enthusiasm in you that will sharpen your senses, fire up your feelings and make you feel compelled to get things done. You will do it not only for what it will do for you, but because you believe it is something really worthwhile. When Muhammad Ali stepped into the ring to fight, he was not only fighting his opponent: he was fighting racial oppression. If you struggle to muster enthusiasm or get yourself into action, chances are you have chosen the wrong goal. Take a step back and make a better choice; you deserve the best, so choose the best.

Develop the Determination to Succeed

Extraordinary people know that if you want to succeed you have got to develop the willingness and desire to work through thick and thin. If your goals are challenging ones, you're going to need plenty of determination to achieve them.

Infuse Your Dreams with Enthusiasm

You can develop this drive and determination by focusing on your future success. What will it look like when you have achieved your goal? What will it feel like? Extraordinary people are excited, passionate, animated and in touch with their feelings. They choose things that they love to do; and they love the feelings that they get while they are doing them.

Have Courage

You have to be prepared to face adversity. You have to resolve to stay on track. You have got to move beyond what other people think and stay true to yourself and your goal.

Be Consistent

Every day offers you another opportunity. You have got to want your goals enough to be prepared to work on them every day, constantly fine-tuning, upgrading, improving and making progress.

Keep Adding to What You Know

You need to be in a constant state of learning. Each day, you need to commit to learning something that moves you closer to your goals, dreams and ambitions.

Be Honest

You need to be brutally honest with yourself. You need to accurately assess where you are, what you need to do and how you need to improve.

Belief in Yourself

If you are not confident, you will need to work on that. If you need help with this, go out and get it. Confidence is not just something you either have or don't have; it's a learnable skill. Optimism is one of the cornerstones of confidence.

Stay Positive

You need to focus on succeeding. You need to think about what you *can* do, not what you can't. You need to bring to mind what is going right, even when some things are going wrong. Always focus on what is possible, rather than what is impossible.

Remain Objective

You need to realise that, as much as your passion will motivate you, it will also colour your opinion. There will be times when you need to make assessments and judgments. It is critical that during these times you can remain objective. You may need to consult your Mastermind Group to help you with this (see page 29).

Learn to Deal with Naysayers

There will always be someone who thinks they know better and will be more than happy to try to bring you down. Realise that this is a part of life and that they are probably criticising your dreams because they are not pursuing their own.

Take Calculated Risks

Extraordinary people often take chances. The difference is that they work out the odds in advance. So if they fail, they accept that at least they have done their best. Get used to working out possibilities inside your mind before you take action. If they don't go to plan after that, simply learn from your mistakes and move on.

Seek Out New Opportunities

Extraordinary people are go-getters: they do not wait for the mountain to come to them, they go to the mountain! They know that life takes on a different pace when you seek out opportunities, rather than waiting for them to come to you. In every moment, you get to choose. You can let life happen to you or you can make it flow through you.

Develop Your People Skills

No man is an island and on your journey to greatness you will need to have friends. It makes sense to develop healthy relationships with people.

Improve Your Communication Skills

Because they are learning and researching all the time, extraordinary people tend to be articulate. This helps them to communicate their ideas and to say the right thing at the right time. In his inaugural address, Nelson Mandela quoted Marianne Williamson to great effect:

> Our deepest fear is not that we are inadequate. Our deepest fear is that we are powerful beyond measure. It is our light, not our darkness that most frightens us. We ask ourselves, Who am I to be brilliant, gorgeous, talented, fabulous? Actually, who are you *not* to be?

Learn the Art of Persuasion

Extraordinary people understand that not everyone is on the same page as them. There are times when you will need to sell your idea or enlist the co-operation of others to help you succeed. You need to develop your powers of ethical persuasion.

Be Nice to Others

If you are about to do extraordinary things, it makes sense to make friends and the best way to do that is to be friendly. Extraordinary people are happy in solitude but they also enjoy the company of others and see the value in making deep and meaningful connections. It is rarely done deliberately, but often it is through these authentic, deep connections that extraordinary people get things done.

Work on Being Patient

Success comes to those who wait. Patience is a virtue. Rome wasn't built in a day. You get the idea! Mahatma Gandhi displayed great patience with his promotion of non-violent protest and eventually he became one of the central figures in securing India's independence.

Keep High Standards

Extraordinary people hold themselves to exceptionally high standards and realise that this is the cornerstone of brilliance. My friend Tom Ziglar is the son of legendary motivational speaker Zig Ziglar. Tom once told me that his dad could do a practice session lasting up to four hours on a speech that he had already delivered hundreds and hundreds of times. Obviously, he was forever tweaking and perfecting; and if you ever hear him speak, you will hear an extraordinary master at work.

See the Funny Side of Things

Extraordinary people don't sweat the small stuff and in the midst of pursuing their goals they realise that it is important to bring fun into all that you do. Enjoy life, discover what you love to do – and do more of it! His Holiness the Dalai Lama is a man with a great sense of humour. A reporter once asked him what he thought of Western civilization; the Dalai Lama smiled and replied: 'I think it would be a great idea!' On another occasion, he was on a formal visit and didn't recognise someone that he should have; he smiled and apologised by saying: 'I am sorry but all you Westerners look the same!'

Be Flexible

Be prepared to make changes and try new things. Extraordinary people realise that, in order to stay ahead of the game, you must accept that the only constant is change. If you change, you grow.

Be Curious

Extraordinary people have an insatiable curiosity. They are perpetually questioning assumptions and experimenting with things. They look for patterns and they examine differences. They are constantly on the lookout for the obscure, the new and the undiscovered.

Develop Your Mental Abilities

Being extraordinary requires mental fitness. Successful people, in their quest for knowledge, realise that it is the brain that processes all of their ideas and stores all of their acquired knowledge. So they spend time learning how to use their brain by working on their thinking skills, creativity and problem-solving. This book is largely dedicated to helping you develop and improve upon these skills.

Develop Your Powers of Concentration

Extraordinary people continually develop their ability to concentrate. They can focus single-mindedly on one question, problem or goal at a time, to the exclusion of all other diversions or distractions. They understand that the more intensely you concentrate your thoughts and your attention, the more emotionally invested you become. In this way, your mind is more likely to respond with the kind of creative ideas that you need for the task at hand.

Tap into the Power of Your Imagination

Extraordinary people realise the power of imagination. Most of them spend time each day using their mind to come up with new ideas, solve problems, create opportunities and develop plans and strategies. They realise that everything comes from the mind; so, the better you can use yours, the greater your chances of success. Shakespeare, Mozart, William Blake, Nikola Tesla and Tchaikovsky all credited their imaginations for the creation of their works of art.

Learn How to Solve Problems

Extraordinary people ensure they have a number of resources available to them to solve problems. These resources can be specialist groups, think tanks, advisers or simply their own insight and intuition.

Exercise: Use Your Subconscious for Problem-Solving

Use your subconscious to come up with solutions to your problems. Have you ever noticed that we often arrive at solutions to problems when we have stopped thinking consciously about them? Use the technique below to tap into the problem-solving power of your subconscious.

1. Find a pen and some paper.
2. Write down what your problem is, giving as much detail as possible.
3. Avoid working on the solution.
4. Remain calm and be as objective as you possibly can.
5. Read your problem aloud.
6. Ask your subconscious to get to work on it.
7. Now close your notepad and do something completely different!

8. Resolve not to put any more conscious thought into your problem for a few days.

9. If the solution to your problem has not come to you within a few days, reopen your notepad and repeat the process.

10. You will find that the solution will flash into your mind when you least expect it. Keep your notebook handy so that you can capture it!

CHAPTER 3

Tapping Into Uncommon Sense

If you want to lead an extraordinary life,
find out what the ordinary do – and don't do it.
Tommy Newberry

Can you imagine what it would be like to run a marathon with nothing in the tank but the power of your positive thoughts? Can you imagine the thrill of getting all psyched up, tensing your muscles, clenching your fists and doing your stretches? 'C'mon man, you can do this. You're a winner! You were born to succeed! Live life to the max!' Your heart beats faster; your determination is in full swing. You burst out the front door in your brand new running gear, iPod strapped to your arm, 'Eye of the Tiger' ringing in your ears. 'What a day for a victory! One day I will look back on this as one of my finest moments. The moment when, through sheer willpower and mental focus, not only did I run a marathon, but I broke the universal galactic record for the fastest moving object in history. Yeah, that's what I'm talking about!'

Two minutes in, you're eating up road and the sweat is streaming down your face. Three minutes in, you're losing your breath but your mind is strong. 'Positive mental attitude! PMA! PMA! PMA all the way! You can do this! You *are* doing this!' Four minutes in, you start to feel lightheaded. It suddenly feels as if your side has been ripped open with a dagger. This is the worst stitch you have ever experienced! Somehow, you soldier on.

You're coming up to the five-minute mark now and your legs are starting to wobble. You feel a dribble coming from your mouth and your face is a grimace with the effort of it all. Flailing arms, shortness of breath, over-heating, lack of oxygen – and all of it happening at the same time. Before you know it, your body slams onto the tarmac; you collapse in sheer exhaustion. Your ankle feels sore. You grab hold of it, writhing in pain. 'Oh man ... now I can't do it! If it weren't for this bloody ankle, I would've knocked it out of the park! Ah well, perhaps another day ... Maybe next week. I'll definitely do it then, when my ankle doesn't hurt so badly. Hopefully it will be better by next week. Maybe ...'

You wouldn't dream of taking on a marathon without training. If you are going to take on a challenge, it makes sense to prepare. If you want to get fit, you prepare your body. If you want to succeed, it makes sense that you train your mind. We can say that success is down to luck, genes or heritage, but there are too many people that keep on disproving those theories. There is a difference between mediocrity and excellence: it comes down to *how we use our minds*.

In this chapter, I want to explain to you how your mind works and how to get it to work for you so that you can lay the foundations of excellence. You can design the life of your dreams and start to move beyond the theory, bringing the extraordinary into your everyday life. Neuro-Linguistic Programming (NLP) can help you to live an extraordinary life. It is the study of how you think, feel, behave and influence others. It involves exploration of three elements:

1. Your brain and how it works.
2. Language (including non-verbal) and how it works.
3. Your ability to combine both of these elements and alter your behaviour so that you can make an impact on your own life and the lives of others.

The giveaway is in the title, really:
- 'Neuro' refers to your brain.
- 'Linguistic' refers to language.
- 'Programming' refers to behaviour.

NLP came out of the study of the patterns of successful people. It uncovered what these people had in common and it put those findings into a system, which could be learned and replicated by others. Researchers in the field of NLP have investigated all areas of personal and interpersonal influence. As a result, NLP offers a number of useful and practical tools and techniques for achieving success. This has revolutionised our ability to achieve excellence through changing how we think, feel and behave.

NLP is underpinned by a number of assumptions:
- Everyone has the ability to change.

- Changing *how* a person thinks is far more effective than changing what a person thinks.
- All of the distinctions that we make in our world come through our five senses.
- People deserve to be treated with respect.
- Behaviour is what we do; it is not who we *are*.
- There is a positive intention behind every behaviour.
- All behaviour is an achievement. There is no such thing as failure if you take the view that failure is feedback.
- You cannot *not* communicate.
- The meaning of your communication is dictated by the response that you get.
- The person with the most flexibility will get the best results.

From the perspective of NLP, you make sense of your world through the use of your five senses:

- You look and see what is in your world.
- You listen and hear what is in your world.
- You touch and feel what is in your world
- You smell what is in your world.
- You taste what is in your world.

These senses work from the outside in and the inside out. Right this moment, light waves from the words on this page are striking your eyes. If you listen, you will hear sounds in your surroundings. You will notice the temperature of the room and any smells that are there. All of this comes from the outside in; and once you are affected by it, you *respond* to it. This response is internally generated: it comes from the inside out. So senses can work from the outside in and the inside out.

However, this is not as clear-cut as it sounds. You do not openly experience all that is happening to you without distinctions. These distinctions prevent you from getting overwhelmed by the masses of information coming at you in any single moment. They allow you to make sense of your environment and to gain a sense of control in your surroundings. If you couldn't make these distinctions, you wouldn't be able to tell a window from a wall or a person from a background. It would all be one big mass of light and energy – and it would be overwhelming.

In the world of NLP, these distinctions are called *filters*. These filters operate across the board. They form our attitudes, values, beliefs, decisions and memories. They ultimately determine how we concentrate, learn, think and create. This, in turn affects how we view and respond to the world. There are three of these filters and they are responsible for the *Deletion*, *Distortion* and *Generalisation* of incoming information. Every piece of incoming information gets reinterpreted as it is being experienced. This can lead to difficulty or opportunity, depending on the way we store the information.

It is because of these filters that when you look, it is not always without prejudice. When you hear, it is not always without choice. When you feel, it is not always without judgment. So, if you want to reach new heights and break new ground, new skills must be learned. You must learn how to look and to see, to really see more of what is there and what has gone unnoticed before. You must learn how to listen and to hear, to really hear beyond what you expect to hear. In this way, you will experience a greater richness, encounter deeper revelations and enjoy sensual intricacies. You will find newer, truer, more complete forms of self- expression. This is how you can move from the ordinary to the *extraordinary*. You can choose to live an exceptional life: a life full of promise, a life full of surprises, a life full of challenge, a life full of progress, a life that will give to you far more than you could ever give to it.

The skills that you are about to learn are exactly the skills used by the successful people modelled to create NLP. These are tools that will help create your blueprint for success. As you use this book, keep in mind that you are not expected to master any of these skills in one sitting. Rome wasn't built in a day. The good news is that each small piece that you *do* master can make a huge difference in your life. So take the skills, practise the skills, output the skills and revisit the skills. Be patient, be diligent and get ready for those exhilarating moments when you notice them working! Every so often your life will sparkle – and when it does, you will have risen to a new level. Your mission, should you choose to accept it, is to increase the amount of sparkle until your life positively shimmers with it

Making Sense of Things

One of the first things extraordinary people learn to master is also one of the most basic things; well, five of them actually. Extraordinary people learn how to fine-tune their sensory skills. Why? Because this is the palette on which you will create your masterpiece.

You may have heard the following expression: 'Whatever the mind can conceive, the mind can achieve.' Think of your senses as the cornerstones of greatness. These are the shoulders on which goals and dreams are carried. You can point your consciousness wherever you like, but you need to have strong foundations first.

Exercise: Sensory Acuity

This three-part exercise will make you much more aware of your senses.

Part One

This will take just 5–10 seconds.
1. Close your eyes.
2. Think of someone you love.
3. Keep the thought in your mind for a few moments.
4. Notice what you notice.
5 Open your eyes.

Part Two

1. What did you see?
2. What did you hear?
3. What did you feel?
4. What did you smell?
5. What did you taste?

Now, repeat the exercise, taking a little longer this time. Try 15–20 seconds, then open your eyes again.

Part Three

Record your experience in the chart below.

Whatever your recollection was, this is your starting point. It doesn't matter whether you could see a clear picture or not. It doesn't matter whether you had a picture but no sound. It doesn't even matter if all you had was a vague feeling. This is something you may not be used to doing but it is a skill that you will need to develop to increase your chances of success. What you are doing here is bringing a process that is normally automatic and unconscious into your everyday awareness. The reason you are doing that is so that you can learn to develop it and gain more control over it.

Activity	Description
What did you see?	
What did you hear?	
What did you feel?	
What did you smell?	
What did you taste?	

Exercise: Mind Movie

Let's bring the last exercise to a new level so that you can build on your skills. This exercise will also be done in three parts.

Part One

This time, I would like you to think about something that you want to *achieve*. You could think about an extraordinary goal or you could imagine what it would be like to be living an extraordinary life. Recall the questions from the last exercise and use them to prompt yourself. Do this as naturally and effortlessly as possible.

1. Close your eyes to limit any external distractions.
2. Bring your goal to mind and indulge in it for a few moments.
3. Take a little time to allow it to build inside your mind.
4. Allow it to build further by placing your attention on it.
5. If your mind wanders, bring your attention back to your goal.

All you are doing here is thinking. This is not a meditation exercise or anything like it. What I am asking you to do is to imagine a personal goal and to spend a few moments thinking about it. Once you have spent time thinking about it, you will have built a memory of it. Now make a written record of it.

Description of My Extraordinary Mind Movie

Part Two

Now that you have described your movie, I want you to return to thinking about your goal. This time, I am not interested in the content of your movie; I want to know about the *sensory qualities* of your movie.

It might help you to think of a TV set. The same movie will appear different depending on the TV set it is viewed on. A large-screen TV will produce a better viewing experience than a small TV. High-definition TV will give a sharper picture.

I want you to concentrate on the experience that your five senses are producing. Your five senses are like the controls on the TV: sometimes you need to adjust them to enhance your overall viewing experience. With that in mind, I want you to run your mind movie again.

Answer the questions below (ignoring the Best Response column for now). You may need to close your eyes a few times and refocus to answer all the questions.

Picture Quality	Question	Answer	Best Response
Colour	Is your movie in colour or black and white?		
Clarity	Is the picture focused or unfocused?		
Size	What size is it, relative to real life?		
Shape	What shape is it?		
Quantity	How many images do you see?		
Location	Where is it? If you were to point at it, where would you point?		
Distance	How far away is it?		
Motion	Is it a movie or a still picture?		
Frame	Has it got a border or is it borderless?		
Format	Is it in 3D or 2D?		
Dissociated	Can you see yourself in the image?		
Associated	Are you looking through your own eyes in the image?		

Sound Quality	Question	Answer	Best Response
Volume	Is it loud or quiet?		
Quality	Is it harsh or soothing?		
Pitch	Is it high, medium or low in range?		
Rhythm	Does it have a beat to it?		
Continuity	Is it constant or irregular?		
Direction	From which direction does the sound come?		
Location	Is the sound clearer in one ear than the other?		

Quality of Feeling	Question	Answer	Best Response
Intensity	How strong is the feeling?		
Location	Where in your body do you feel it?		
Quality	Does it feel heavy or light?		
Direction	If it moves, where does it move to?		
Speed	How fast does it travel?		
Duration	Is it constant or irregular?		
Type	Does it come in waves or does it pulse in and out?		

Smells and Tastes	Question	Answer	Best Response
Aromatic	Is there an aroma or strong smell to it?		
Fragrant	Is there a fragrance or perfume to it?		
Bitter	Is there a bitter taste to it?		
Sweet	Is there a sweet taste to it?		
Salty	Is there a salty taste to it?		
Sour	Is there a sour taste to it?		

For most people, the senses of smell and taste are not as highly developed as other senses. Some people need very strong senses of smell and taste for their professions, e.g. wine tasters or chefs. For most people, though, these senses are somewhat underdeveloped. While all of our senses are important, for the purposes of NLP, most people experience great improvements by working only with seeing, hearing and feeling.

Part Three

Now that you have described the sensory qualities of your movie, you can explore further by examining your own answers, thinking about alternative answers and seeing which of these answers elicits the *strongest positive response* from you.

Examine the first answer you gave in the first chart, regarding **colour**. If you originally imagined your movie in *black and white*, think about it again. This time, imagine it in *colour*. Simply ask yourself to imagine what it would look like – your brain will respond. This might take a few attempts but stick with it.

As soon as you can see your movie in colour, notice how that makes you *feel*. You are checking to see if you can elicit a *stronger positive response* from yourself. When you change the movie from black and white to colour, does it feel like an improvement? If it does, write 'colour' for Best Response.

Now, work on finding Best Response to the **clarity** of your movie. If you originally imagined your movie as *blurry and unfocused*, think about it again. Imagine it as *clear and focused*. Which version gives you the best response? (It is likely that the clearer and more focused the picture, the stronger your response to it.)

Bear in mind that there may be elements that don't need changing. Let's say that your initial movie had a frame around it and you notice that, in removing the frame, the feeling diminishes. Then you know what to do: keep it there because it works best for you! You may also discover that by adjusting one element the whole movie may change or even disappear. This is perfectly fine. If that happens, just begin again and avoid changing that particular element the next time.

Work through all of your answers in this way. By the end of this exercise, you will have a much clearer idea of the best viewing experience for you. In future, when you visualise a goal, you will know how to adjust the setting to get your best viewing experience.

Animator and producer Walt Disney was the father of the process known as storyboarding. If he was to do a Mind Movie, there would be little need for adjustment! He was known for having a powerful use of all of his senses. This made him the vibrant character he was and helped him to come up with such fantastic ideas for cartoons. Now, you don't need to be Walt Disney to create your own Mind Movie but it's nice to remind yourself just how powerful the human brain can be.

The Nikola Tesla Method

Nikola Tesla used his strong powers of imagination in creating new inventions:

'I do not rush into actual work. When I get an idea I start at once building it up in my imagination. I change the construction, make improvements and operate the device in my mind ... In this way I am able to rapidly develop and perfect a conception without touching anything. When I have gone so far as to embody in the invention every possible improvement I can think of and see no fault anywhere, I put into concrete form this final product of my brain. Invariably my device works as I conceived that it should, and the experiment comes out exactly as I planned it.'

The Difference that Makes the Difference

Whatever you allow to form in your mind is going to have an effect on your subconscious. Your subconscious is the mind that gets things done. The quality of the formation will determine your emotional response and the strength of your emotional response will determine whether that formation is a memory that becomes an *instruction* or simply a *memory* that is stored away. This is the difference that makes the difference. The bigger, brighter, clearer and more lifelike the image, the more power it has to imprint on your mind. The same goes for all of the other senses. The more true to life they feel, the more powerful their effect will be. The quality of your pictures and sounds will have a direct bearing on the strength of your feelings; and your feelings act as the messenger. If the message is weak, the response will be weak. If it is too weak, the experience will be stored as a memory. If the message is powerful, it will be stored as both a *memory* and an *instruction*.

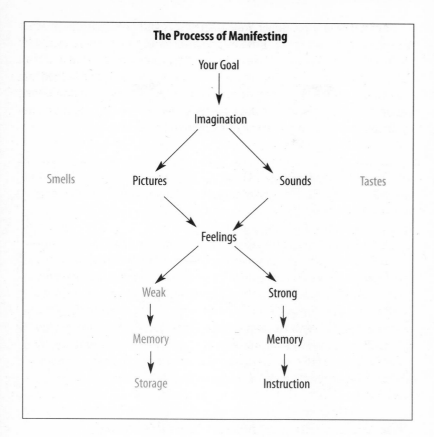

The Movie Room

Many successful people build a construct inside their minds to help them with this process of manifestation. Memory experts swear by these kinds of mental constructs. If you find it helpful, you can design your own 'laboratory of the mind' or 'mental palace'. Personal development guru Maxwell Maltz called it the 'theatre of the mind'. I call it the Movie Room.

The idea is simple: you create a space in your mind and you use it regularly for your imaginings. You can design your own control panel to help you remember the qualities that may need adjusting as you work on your goals. At our seminars, we ask delegates to design their own mental control panels for adjusting the qualities of their senses. You should see what they come up with! There are panels with levers, push buttons, switches, flashing lights and all sorts of controls.

The idea of a Movie Room in your mind might seem elaborate but it actually works. I like to place my goal on a screen in front of me and watch it play through. I see it from the outside first, then I step in and out of the movie so that I can feel the experience fully and make it more lifelike. Each time I do this I layer the experience by telling myself how much fun it will be while I am doing it and when it is done.

When the time comes for me to achieve this goal in real life, I stay motivated by reminding myself that even if it is stressful at times, I am doing this because I enjoy it. I remember that it is all of my own making and I can change it any time I want. Trying to achieve bigger goals will require extra maintenance. So, if I am working towards a major goal, I visit the Movie Room frequently. I also do progress reports, examine my feelings and focus on the end goal.

I have realised that enthusiasm has to be managed. At times, it makes me want to do too much. So sometimes I need to pull in the reins, sit with the good feelings, place my goal in the background and remember that I am still human after all. Think about the marathon runner at the start of this chapter. Enthusiasm is great – but it has to be channelled properly. You have got to keep it real if you are in this for the long haul!

However you choose to manifest your goals, do it often. Try visiting the Movie Room daily, on first waking up or when you are going to sleep. Both of these times are powerful, as your brain is shifting towards the alpha state, which is ideal for mental programming. Whenever you choose to do this work, remember that it is vital to be *patient*. Things do not have to run perfectly. Your aim is to get the positive feelings flowing – so everything you do should focus on that. Remaining curious, open and adventurous will be a great help.

Even the smallest changes can have powerful results. So don't worry if it takes lots of practice to master the controls of your Movie Room. You will soon learn how to make many changes of picture, sound, etc. Learning these skills will have a huge influence on your behaviour.

Sensory Preferences

In really tuning in to our senses, we can discover which ones give us the strongest emotional responses. You might wonder how all this mind work can impact on your real life, but finding out about your sensory preferences can tell you an awful lot about *how your mind works*.

Read the statements below. They reveal a lot about the sensory preferences of the speaker.

Pictures

- I don't understand what you are saying to me; I just can't get the picture!
- Give me some time to think about it; it appears a little hazy to me at the minute.
- Now you are blowing this way out of proportion!
- Right now I really need to get some distance from my problems.
- It's pretty black and white to me.
- It's beginning to shape up nicely now.
- I have just had a flash of inspiration!

Sounds

- Sounds okay to me.
- That's loud and clear!
- Tone it down a bit, will you?
- It's like things have come to a screeching halt.

Feelings

- I am under a bit of pressure at the minute.
- It's a weight off my mind.
- I am cool as a cucumber.
- You're looking hot today!
- My head is in a bit of a spin at the moment.

Smells

- Life just stinks right now.
- Something smells 'off' here.

Tastes

- It left a bitter taste in my mouth.
- Ah, the sweet taste of success!

The evidence of how our brains work is all around us, so why is it that so many people don't get the great results they crave? It comes back to the *filters* mentioned earlier: Deletion, Distortion and Generalisation. Your brain is constantly looking for and creating patterns. These patterns form habits and these habits form limitations in our thinking. In a nutshell, your brain takes the easy way out. It finds something that works and it creates a habit based on that.

Doing the sensory skills exercises in this chapter will have given you evidence of how your brain works and what your sensory preferences are. Continue to take note of your everyday behaviours and language: they will reveal many clues about your preferences.

Identifying Sensory Preferences

Sight

If sight is your preference you sometimes might judge a person by how they look. You might literally judge a book by its cover! Business tycoon and TV personality Peter Jones has admitted that he is turned on or off by the way people look. When a person enters the room, the first thing he does is look them up and down. That look is the make-or-break point of many a pitch to him on *Dragons' Den*. He has commented in interviews that there are two kinds of people he would never invest in: dishonest or scruffy people. That gives you some indication of how highly he values appearances. You will notice that he is always impeccably dressed himself; there is never a hair out of place. He is neat, tidy and orderly. I expect that his personal workspace is, too.

It's likely that sight is your preference if you often say, 'Look at me when I'm talking to you!' You literally look to understand, so you consider eye contact very important. Do you often drift into a daydream because you get so wrapped up in the movie inside your mind? Do you have problems remembering long verbal instructions?

People with a preference for sight will make statements similar to these:
- The way it appears to me is ...
- Well, aren't you a sight for sore eyes?
- I have taken a dim view on that.
- Let's take a bird's-eye view of it.
- I have an image of it in my mind's eye.
- The future is looking bright.
- Now, that's a horse of a different colour.
- I just caught a glimpse of him when he was passing.

- Would you like to take a peek?
- I don't want to make a scene.
- I think that was very short-sighted of him.
- She is as pretty as a picture.
- In hindsight, I can see that.
- That is true beyond a shadow of a doubt.

Do you see what I mean?

Below are some other words that indicate a preference for sight.

Bright   Focus   Foresight   Hindsight
Preview   Outlook
Light   Review
Vision   Illustrate
Scope   Scene   Show   Appear
View   Look
Demonstrate   Overview   Pinpoint
Sketch

Possible Indicators of a Preference for Sight

Body Type:	Either thin or obese.
Posture:	Erect, straight with head and shoulders up.
Gesture:	Jerky, finger-pointing, hand over the face.
Eye movements:	Upwards to left and right.
Breathing:	High in the chest.
Speech:	High, clear, fast and loud.
Lip size:	Thin and tight.
Career:	Artist, painter, architect, designer or photographer.

Sound

If sound is your preference, you like nothing better than to have a good old natter! If you talk to yourself a lot, you're not mad; you probably just like using your voice. If you love to listen to music, and prefer the radio or iPod to the television, that could also be an indication. As you read this text, are you also speaking it inside your mind? Believe it or not, not everybody does that. Speed-readers just *see* what they read, so it's obvious the category to which they belong. If, on the other hand, you find your lips moving as you read, you probably have a preference for sound.

People with a preference for sound will make statements similar to these:

- John? Yeah, he's sound.
- That name rings a bell with me.
- He is a real chatterbox, a total blabbermouth.
- I am after getting an awful earful from Tom about it.
- Pay attention when I am speaking, will you?
- State your reasons for saying that.
- You have me all tongue-tied at this stage.
- To tell the truth …
- Sorry, I just tuned out there for a second.
- Hold your tongue!
- He is very outspoken.
- In a manner of speaking
- He is a real telltale, that fella!
- This is what he said, word for word
- I am not telling you a word of a lie.

Does that sound about right to you?

Below are some other words that indicate a preference for sound.

Announce   Proclaim   Mention   Communicate
Discuss   Listen   Ring   Hear
Say   Roar   Noise   Hush   Earshot
Rumour   Tone   Voice   Screech

> ## Possible Indicators of a Preference for Sound
> Body Type: Inconsistent.
> Posture: Head tilted to the side, touching or pointing to ear.
> Gesture: Clicking fingers, tapping, touching mouth and chin.
> Eye movements: Across left and right, and down to left.
> Breathing: Mid-section of the chest.
> Speech: Resonant and rhythmic.
> Lip size: Varies.
> Career: Musician, presenter or sales.

Feeling

If you are one of those people who likes to dress for comfort and thinks it's important to take your time with things, then you most likely have a preference for feeling. If the thoughts of being snuggled up and cosy by the fire excite you, that's also an indication. Do you speak a little slower than other people? Do you ever rub your lap as you speak? If you think it's important that everyone gets in touch with their feelings, you are definitely ranking higher on the scale for a preference for feelings. If you like group hugs, I'd nearly bet on you having the preference. Do you feel overwhelmed when you encounter beauty or someone shows you kindness? Are you the first to reach for the tissues when you watch a sad movie? Chances are, you have a preference for feeling.

People with a preference for feeling will make statements similar to these:

- Now hold it a minute!
- Let's start from scratch.
- You've just got to go with the flow.
- Get a load of this!
- Sorry, it must have slipped my mind.
- Hang on in there; it will be fine.
- Now *that* was a stroke of good luck!
- It's just too much hassle; I couldn't be bothered about it.
- Don't go losing the head now.
- He lost his shirt on it.
- What it all boils down to is …

- Could you give me a hand with this, please?
- Are you catching my drift?
- That strikes me as a good approach.

Are you getting a handle on this stuff now?

Below are some other words that indicate a preference for feeling.

Firm   Hold   Swift
Feel
Handle   Impact
Touch   Strike
Impress
Sharpen   Tangible   Warmth   Cold
Stress   Sense   Grip   Grasp

Possible Indicators of a Preference for Feeling

Body Type:	Soft, full, rounded or loose.
Posture:	Head partially tilted or facing downwards to the right.
Gesture:	Self-soothing, occasionally touching the body (stomach, chest, hands or lap).
Eye movements:	Down to right.
Breathing:	Deep, full and low in the stomach.
Speech:	Slow, with pauses.
Lip size:	Full and soft.
Career:	Therapist, sculptor, engineer or body builder.

Smell and Taste

People's senses of smell and taste are usually not as developed as the other senses, so a preference for smell or taste is not as common. For that reason, I'll combine these categories.

People with a preference for smell or taste will make statements similar to these:

- Smells fishy to me...
- This stinks!

- That was a bitter pill to swallow.

Below are some other words that indicate a preference for smell or taste.

Bitter   Bland   Delicious   Appetising

Sweet   Sour   Spicy   Salty   Musty

Tasty   Tangy   Flavoursome   Odour

Stench   Smells

Bouquet   Stink   Reeks   Fragrant   Aroma

The Eyes Have It!

Our sensory preferences are revealed through our language and gestures, but eye movements are also very important. In NLP, these are called Eye Accessing Cues. Your brain is like a filing cabinet: it has certain places for certain things. If you want to imagine or remember something, there is a specific place in which that is done. When you recall a memory, talk to yourself or are consumed by a feeling, your eyes go in a very specific direction. People move their eyes all over the place but these movements are not random. They are evidence that you are accessing different parts of the brain.

Remember that these movements happen in a flash and you can access many different parts of the brain in one quick sequence. I could ask you to remember what you had for lunch yesterday and, at the same time, to try to imagine that when you were eating your lunch, Will Smith arrived at your door – dressed in a purple suit – and asked you for a loan of a fiver. Quite a lot going on there! Your eyes would move in many directions during this mental process. They would go: up to the left to remember seeing yourself; across right to imagine yourself licking a spoon; mid-range to the left again to remember what Will Smith's voice sounded like; then across to the right to imagine what he would sound like asking for a fiver. If you thought the whole exercise was silly, your eyes would dip down right; if you talked to yourself about how silly it all was, they would dip down left.

A lot happens in a few moments but if you pay attention you will start to notice these patterns. A good way to study this is to watch an interview on TV with the volume on mute. See if you can work out what the person is doing. Are they talking about pictures, sounds or feelings? Have fun with it!

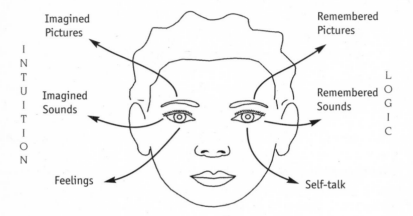

Did you know that the reason most people spell poorly is because they are sounding out the words? Words are pictures, so when we learn them it is best to study the word, avoid sounding it out, then picture it in your mind. It will help if you raise your eyes slightly and look up left as you do this. This is where the word will later be stored in your brain. The *slowest* way to learn the spelling of the word is through sounding it out but most teachers are not aware of that.

Using the information in this chapter, you will learn how to master the workings of your own mind. In Chapter 4, you will learn how to win the hearts and minds of other people.

Creating Extraordinary Relationships

You will get all you want in life if
you help enough other people get what they want.
Zig Ziglar

If you want to live an extraordinary life, it makes sense to learn as much as you can about getting on with people. Most of our feelings of self-worth come from the quality of the relationships that we have with the people around us. No matter what people teach you about being independent and being in control of your feelings, you wouldn't be human if other people never affected you. In fact, life wouldn't be worth living if we didn't have relationships with other people. This chapter will explore the art of relationship-building and influence. The skills that you are about to learn can lift and transform your relationships with your loved ones, work colleagues and even the people that you have just met.

In researching this book, I delved deep into all the personality theories that I could find. I waded through book after book – and ended up right back where I started. The most effective and dependable skills, as well as the ones most capable of predicting behaviour, come from the field of NLP.

The Importance of Empathy

In Chapter 3, I introduced the idea of sensory-based preferences and demonstrated that these preferences can be revealed in a number of ways, particularly through our everyday language. Getting to know these preferences allows you to understand how people are communicating with you and themselves.

Cast your mind back to Chapter 1 and you will remember that the first Human Fulfilment Want is *empathy*. One of the most precious gifts you can give to another person is the gift of empathy, that ability to demonstrate understanding. Mutual understanding is the foundation of any healthy relationship and when you are able to convey that to another person you are setting in place the opportunity to create more meaningful connections.

Creating empathy with another person also creates an environment where you will have the ability to influence that person. We are all influencing one another all of the time. And the best way we can influence one another is when we come to it with the *correct intentions*. Think about the Zig Ziglar quote at the beginning of this chapter and you will understand what is meant by 'influence'.

Creating Rapport

If you can show someone that you understand them, you create a connection with that person. Once you create a connection with them and establish a degree of trust, then you have a rapport. Rapport is what happens when you are in harmony with another person; you are on the same page, so to speak. The ability to create and maintain rapport with the people you meet is one of the most powerful skills you will ever acquire. Some people appear to have it naturally. His Holiness the Dalai Lama has an incredible ability to make someone he has just met feel like they are the most important person in the room. Apparently, Bill Clinton has this ability, too. Rapport has something to do with the fact that we tend to like people who like us. People who easily build rapport appear to have a personal charisma or presence that immediately affects people. Most of us put that down to an innate characteristic or gift – something that one is born with – but this is not the case.

Charm, presence and the ability to create a deep and meaningful connection with a person that you have just met are actually skills; and those skills come from your ability to establish rapport. This is not something that exists inside of you: it is something that you *do*. It is a behaviour, or rather a set of behaviours, which you are now going to learn.

Rapport is that ability to demonstrate understanding, to establish a meaningful connection and to create a feeling of total acceptance of the other person. You will always know whether it is present or absent by the way you are feeling. When it is present, you feel comfortable, connected and well. When it is absent, you feel uncomfortable, disconnected and not so well.

Rapport is a Process

Although rapport is a skill, it is not really something that you *do* to somebody: it is something that you *create* between you and the other person. The establishment of rapport is an organic process and it depends on the mutual consent of both parties. Once you have it, you can keep it by constantly remaining aware of the emotional needs of both parties. When I say both parties, of course there can be more than two. You can have rapport with a group, an audience, even a nation. You can actually be in rapport with any living being that is sentient. Rapport is all about the *relationship* you are having with the other person. We can go in and out of rapport many times, even in a single conversation; that is natural. The more you have in common with someone, the more likely you are to find yourself naturally in rapport with them most of the time. This is because we like people who are like us. Rapport has to be created, maintained and sometimes reintroduced.

Permission to Connect

When you communicate with someone, you get to stand at the gateway of their world. You earn the right to become involved in that world on the basis of two principles: first, that you improve it; and second, that you do not upset it. These two principles form the backdrop to every human interaction.

Your every word, action and gesture goes under the radar when you are in a relationship with someone. This is what causes a person to blow hot or cold in an instant. Because of our social conditioning, there will be plenty of times when a person has not left our company physically, but they have left it psychologically and emotionally, because our rapport with them is broken. Your job is to be able to pull them back on board when it matters, if it matters. The fact that you operate under the same principles as they do, makes you continuously aware of that hold; and the cold feeling that comes when rapport is damaged. This gives you the ability to know when to adjust, if necessary.

Obviously, there will be times in any communication where there will be a level of tension or disagreement and that's fine; that is natural. But there are also times when rapport can be really damaged and we need to be aware during those times. Times, for example, when you bark at your partner and you need to put that right; times when you need another person's co-operation in order to get something done; or times when you really want to create a connection. We will need to create connections for different reasons: sometimes we want to start a relationship; sometimes we want to motivate a person; sometimes we want to sell an idea or product to a person and we need to earn the right to stay in their company.

If we can keep things running smoothly in our relationships, both parties can get what they want from the interaction. In this way, we can influence each other by reacting appropriately when things take a detour, or by creating the circumstances that will keep the relationship on track in tough times.

Setting the Pace

It is vital to set pace with the person you wish to connect with. Pacing simply means *matching*; the principle being that if you look, sound and behave like the other person, they will feel that you like and understand them and they will be comfortable with you. If you get your intentions right, you will not need to pace people very often: their intuition will tell them that your intentions are good and that you mean them no harm. However, not everyone will be as tuned in with you as you might like. For this reason, you may have to work a little to help nudge your natural charm along the way.

If you need to pace someone, the best way to pace them is to match behaviours that are typically outside their awareness. When matching behaviours, it is subtlety, similarity and moderation that are key. Below are some examples of pacing.

Breathing

You can adjust your breathing patterns to match the person you wish to connect with: if the person is breathing low and shallow, you can do likewise. Be careful not to go overboard, though: if you alter your own breathing too dramatically, you will feel weird and that will be noticeable. If you normally breathe high and shallow in your chest, your best bet is to gradually shift your breathing to the middle of your chest, and then into your lower abdomen. If you do this, it will not only alter your breathing, it will alter your thinking and even the rate of your speech. If that's what you want to do – brilliant! You have established the connection. You are now in their world. However, you must always keep in mind *why* you have chosen to enter their world. Is it to connect or to influence? If you are there to influence, you need to keep an eye on the bigger picture because, once you have established a connection, you then need to lead the person from their world into yours.

Posture and Gesture

You can also set pace by mirroring the other person's posture. This can be done directly or indirectly; partially or completely. If the other person is sitting back in their chair, you could slowly ease back from the position you are in until you approximate their posture. If they change position, you gradually do the same. If they sit up and move forward to engage with you, do the same in a way that is respectful and unobtrusive. If they fold their arms, you could cross yours. If they tap their foot, you could do what's known as a *cross-over match*, e.g. you match the pace of their tapping by holding a pen in your hand and tapping it quite subtly to the same beat. In everything that you do to set pace, the key is to work outside the other person's awareness. In this way, you will not distract them. If you make this stuff obvious, you may actually offend the other person – and that is no way to build rapport. In the midst of all this, be clear about your intention. Your goal should be to make the other person feel comfortable and good about themselves; that way, you can *both* achieve your goals through mutual respect and co-operation.

Facial Expression

If you pay attention to the facial expressions of another person, you may notice little habits they have; and you can reflect these back at them. Many people aren't really aware of the subtleties in their own facial expressions. Perhaps they scrunch up their nose slightly or raise their eyebrows more than usual when they are amused – and they are completely unaware of these habits. These little nuances make a person unique, so you have to be very careful in mirroring them. Be subtle and respectful – or you run the risk of really offending somebody.

Voice

In Chapter 3, we touched on the fact that each of us has a certain volume, tone, rate and rhythm to our voice. Some people (especially those with a sensory preference for feeling) speak with deep tones at a slow rate, with plenty of pauses. Other people (especially those with a sensory preference for pictures) speak with a sharp tone at a quick rate. If you adjust your own tone, volume, inflections and rate of speech, you can move towards resembling the voice of the other person – and this is very powerful.

Language

If you have ever worked in a large organisation, one of the first things you will notice is that it has language elements unique to the place. If you want to be accepted into the organisation, you need to learn the language pretty quickly or you run the risk of standing out. And most organisations offer very few positions where you are allowed to stand out. Usually, if you are the boss (or next in line to the boss), you are allowed to be eccentric. If you are not, your eccentricities can make you the butt of the office jokes, which is not pleasant.

Being social animals, humans like to feel that we belong to a group. When we belong to a group, we take on its customs and practices. One of the most noticeable ways this happens is in our use of language. When we meet people that speak like us, we take them as being just like us. Whether we realise it or not, we are clued in to certain phrases. If you use the phrases another person uses, they are likely to see you as being in their clique. Sometimes you can get this wrong, though. Have you ever heard an older person trying to fit in with teenagers by using their fashionable phrases? A forty-nine-year-old man using the word 'chillax' is a strange thing to behold because there are just too many other variables out of synch between the two age groups. Mind you, I regularly use youth slang to terrorise and embarrass my own children! I believe that, as an irresponsible parent, you need to do these things every so often – purely because you can.

Sensory Preference

Few people are aware of the way in which their speech reflects how their mind is working in any given moment. They accept that speech reflects *what* they are thinking, but they don't realise that it reflects *how* they are thinking. A really powerful way to establish a more meaningful connection is by way of pacing and matching a person's sensory preferences. These preferences reveal how they habitually think, create, view and respond to the world. It follows then that if you match and pace the way they do this, your capacity to connect and influence begins to skyrocket. This truly sets the foundation for establishing extraordinary relationships.

Sight Preference Statements

If you want to pace a person who has a sensory preference for sight, here's how the conversation might go.

'In **hindsight**, it **appears** to me that no one bothered to take a **look** and **see** if there was anything that could go wrong in the first place. To be honest with you, I have taken a **dim view** of the entire **scenario** all together.'

'I **see** what you mean and from your **perspective** I agree it does **look** that way. If you will allow me, I can **pinpoint** for you exactly what we were **focusing** on at the time it happened, and that will perhaps **shed some more light** on the situation.'

'Okay, well hurry up and **show** me. I have places to go and people to **see!**'

'Sure – let me **paint you a picture** so you will be able to **plainly see** exactly what took place on the night in question.'

Remember, the objective here is to move from a situation of no rapport to one that begins to rebuild it. For that reason, there is no disagreement in the statement. Instead, there is an acceptance of understanding, which is followed by a request to explain the situation. Throughout, there is use of the language preferred by those with a sensory preference for sight.

Sound Preference Statements

'I **hear tell** things didn't go as planned yesterday. Now I am getting an **earful** from the client, which has left me **speechless**. Can you please **tell** me what all the **noise** was about?'

'Yes, you **heard** correctly. I tried to give you a **shout** because I knew that **call** was coming, but your phone was off. If you can please **hear me out**, it won't take a minute. I will **tell** you what happened **word for word**.'

'So what you're **saying** is …'

'Incredible as it all **sounds**, I am not **telling** you **a word** of a lie. But you don't have to take my **word** for it. There was a customer there, too, and he will **tell** you the exact same thing.'

Feeling Preference Statements

'Well if there is one thing that **makes my blood boil**, it is when John Dolan comes **shuffling** into my office, **throwing his weight around**, **breathing down my neck** and **putting pressure on me** because someone was too lazy to **carry out** a few simple tasks last night.'

'I am **sorry** you had to **go through** that and I know you must have **been put in a very uncomfortable situation.** If you **can hang on in there** for just a minute, I will **get to grips** with what **all the hassle** was about. I wasn't there last night and it **slipped my mind** to **check in** and find out how the lads were **getting on** first thing this morning; but I'll **take a trip** over there now and **get to the bottom** of it.'

Pacing to Lead

There will be times when you need to *lead a person from one feeling to another*, e.g. if the person is not co-operating. To get them to open up and co-operate, you simply *pace* and then *lead*. So, once you have established the connection by matching their posture, tone of voice and language, you slowly readjust and begin to move in the direction that you want the other person to be in. If the person is in a bad mood and has their head down, shoulders slumped and is talking in a low voice, you match all of these things and then begin to change them gradually. If you have established rapport, the other person will begin to respond. If they fail to respond, it means you do not have rapport and you need to do more things to establish the rapport. It is only when you have paced the person correctly and made a respectful connection that you can exert your influence and bring about the desired change by leading them to where you want them to go. Obviously, if you move too fast or you move too far, you are in danger of breaking the rapport.

Sensory Suggestions

If you have managed to create a strong rapport, your capacity to influence is increased considerably and the other person will be far more open to your suggestions or advice. You can use the rapport you have gained to exert a positive influence on the other person. Remember, when you say something to another person in order for them to understand you, you have to *try out what you have said* in their own minds. If you use a language that suits their sensory preferences, you will encourage them to open up and to consider your views.

Below are some examples of statements with answers that are suitable to the sensory preferences on display.

Sight

'I don't understand what you are saying to me; I just can't get the **picture**!'
'Okay, I **see** what you mean. Let me explain it again so that you can see it in your **mind's eye**.'

'Give me some time to think about it; it appears a little **hazy** to me at the minute.'
'Sure – take as much time as you like to **focus** and get it **clear** in your mind.'

'Now you are blowing this *way* out of **proportion**.'
'If you could **see** more completely – in **full 3D** – you might have a broader **perspective** on it.'

'Right now I really need to get some **distance** from my problems.'
'Yes, you're probably better of just putting them out of your mind and **focusing** on the good stuff instead.'

'It looks **black and white** to me.'
'Yes, but there many **shades of every colour**.'

'It's beginning to **shape** up nicely now.'
'Brilliant – let's **square** it off and finish it out.'

'I have just had a **flash** of inspiration!'
'Excellent – you will have to **shed some light** on it for me.'

Sound

'**Sounds** okay to me.'
'Yeah, it sure had a good **ring** to it.'

'That's **loud** and clear!'
'I like the **sound** of it, okay!'

'**Tone** it down a bit, will you?'
'**Sound**.'

'It's like things have come to a **screeching** halt.'
'Well, maybe we need to lift the handbrake, get back in the driving seat and make some **noise**!'

Feeling

'I am under a bit of **pressure** at the minute.'
'Hopefully things will begin to ease off now if you give yourself a chance to **blow off some steam**.'

'I can't get this **weight** off my mind.'
'What you need is a little bit of fun; *that* will **lift** it for you.'

'I am **cool** as a cucumber.'
'No, you're not: you're **hot**, hot, hot!'

'You're looking **hot** today.'
'I'm on **fire**!'

'My head is in a bit of a **spin** at the moment.'
'Perhaps you need to **slow** it down a bit, let things **settle** and stop for a moment to **think things through**?'

A Perfect Mismatch

There will be times when it is neither appropriate nor useful to be in rapport with another person. I remember an incident a few months back, when I was sitting in my clinic working on my book. My clinic is beside my home but not connected to it. I had the builders in because I was extending the house at the back, which meant the side gate to the house was left open and anyone could walk in off the road and enter the back garden. I was typing away when I lifted my head from the computer to think for a moment. And there he was: this tall, thin young man with tightly-cut hair, wearing a white tracksuit. He had his back to the wall of the house and he was trying to look as inconspicuous as possible, all the while edging his way forward towards the end of the newly-built extension. Once he got there, he took a few quick peeks around the corner of the wall and in the window, his head jutting forwards and backwards like a hen pecking seeds. He was checking to see if there was anyone in the house. Obviously, he was up to no good.

I got up from my chair, walked up behind him and said, 'Are you alright?' Agitated, he turned to me and said, 'Ah have you any copper, mister?' I looked at him disdainfully (not one of my wisest moments) and signalled for him to leave, saying, 'C'mon ... out!' Within a nanosecond, he was standing in front of me, filling my personal space and screaming at the top his voice. He was a good six inches taller than me, so he was looking down at me as he roared. His eyes bulged, his nostrils flared, his face reddened and his neck was pushed aggressively forward. 'Have you got a problem? Have you got a problem? What are ya sayin'?' He stood there with his legs in the 'A' position and his fists clenched. His arms were at his side but extended, as if he was a cowboy getting ready to draw his guns. Things were happening so fast and I was shocked that a person could get so ferociously angry that quickly. This was nought to insane in the flash of an instant! I felt generally calm, though, and was more curious about his behaviour than threatened by it.

I answered him with a tone much lower than his own (another error) and said, 'Look – you'll have to leave or I'll call the guards.' With that, he nearly lifted from the ground with rage. He was simply seething with anger as he began roaring at me again. His mouth was wide open and I could see his teeth, which looked like they'd endured a few too many hash blowbacks; they were rotting in his head. All the while, I was thinking to myself that he must have grown up in a horribly aggressive home – there was no other explanation for that amount of anger. He got louder and louder: 'Are you gonna call the bleedin' coppers, are ya? Are you gonna call the bleedin' coppers? *Are ya? Are ya?!* Well, go on then! *Call* the bleedin' coppers! I'll bleedin' dance on your head! Ya f***ing b***ard ! Go *on! Call* the bleeding coppers then!' At this point, I was thinking that one of us could get hurt really badly. If I had to hit him, I'd have to make sure he couldn't get back up – or he would *kill* me. If he was to hit *me*, I was done for: he *would* dance on my head.

I took a step back in case he had a knife or a screwdriver. Unknown to me at the time, that was exactly the right thing to do. In his mind, that was a retreat. I spoke, keeping my voice low, unemotional and matter-of-fact in an effort not to connect to his anger: 'Fair enough ... Look – just go.' With that, he turned on his heels, let out a frustrated growl, shook his hands free from the clenched-fist position and began to walk away. As he walked down the path, he became as relaxed and unaffected just as quickly as he had burst into the rage! That just knocked me for six. I had no reference to explain that type of dramatic oscillation in behaviour and it seemed too easy to just put it down to drug use or psychosis.

Months later, I read something that shed a lot of light on this experience. My friend Paul, who is a Krav Maga instructor, posted on his blog a piece all about muggings. Unknown to myself, I had actually done quite a few sensible things during my experience with the raging youth. Paul explained that most muggings are over in about fifteen seconds and he offered some advice on getting through them unharmed. A crucial piece of wisdom was to avoid 'the interview' at all costs. Recall the amount of questions that the aggressive young man put to me during our encounter – this is what Paul calls 'the interview'. Crucially, I never answered any of his questions; I just asked him to leave. Apparently, this is the perfect combination: you avoid engagement and you state what you want in a matter-of-fact way. If I had said that I *was* going to call the guards, that would have been the affirmative that he was looking for. In his mind, he would then have had justification for hitting me.

Attackers often seek justification for their actions before they carry them out. How many times have you heard things like, 'I wouldn't have hit him if he wasn't asking for it!' But even in far less stressful situations, in everyday life, justifications like this can lead to convictions and rationales that drive behaviour. We can learn a lot from studying these things. People say you live and learn; sometimes you learn and live! In truth, though, it wasn't learning that got me out of a dangerous situation; my actions were guided purely by intuition.

I hope that your life remains free of these kinds of negative and volatile encounters. I was fortunate to do enough of the right things to prevent the situation from escalating, but at the time, I wasn't exactly sure that I was doing the right thing. Luckily, I have been in enough emergency situations to know that I tend to react in a calm manner. That is not deliberate; it's just how I respond. I tend to get the 'shock and fear' stuff *after* the event, which sometimes works out nicely for me. Circumstances have given me that insight but it is good to know in advance how you *respond* in times of stress. It is also useful to know how *others respond* because when they do, you can learn how to handle that and bring things back to an even keel.

Virginia Satir's Universal Patterns of Response

Renowned family therapist Virginia Satir identified five universal patterns of response that people resort to under threat. These responses are identifiable through the phrases they involve and the postures that usually accompany them. The overall object of these responses is an attempt to *conceal weakness*.

The Placater

Placaters work to placate so the other person will not get angry or mad at them. They want everyone to remain calm and nobody to get upset. They often say things like, 'Let's all be friends', 'We can all get along if we just work together', etc. Placaters are prepared to give up and give in if it means keeping the peace; *anything* for a peaceful life. They are 'yes men': whatever you want is okay by them.

Perspective:	Agreement.
Feeling Evoked in Others:	Guilt.
Intention:	Spare me.
Body Language:	Head upright, eyebrows raised, palms facing upwards in apologetic mode. Shoulders and hips level, legs slightly apart. Entire body facing forward (including the feet).

The Blamer

Blamers use blame in order to look strong. They want to get rid of the problem by pushing it on someone else. They feel alone, vulnerable, uncared for and powerless. They try to hide this by taking charge of things or bluffing their way through. They deflect from themselves by pointing out the shortcomings of others. They often say things like, 'You never do anything right', 'You're always the same', 'It's all your fault', etc.

Perspective:	Disagreement.
Feeling Evoked in Others:	Fear.
Intention:	Obey me.
Body Language:	Body facing head on and leaning forward. Head down, eyebrows lowered and finger pointing directly at 'the offender'.

The Computer

Computers try to hide behind big words and pretend that there is no real threat at all. They try to project a cool, calm and collected composure; in reality, their emotions may be running havoc underneath the surface. Computers learn to conceal their emotions and view the revealing of emotions as a form of weakness. They compensate by being over-rational. They are cautious, reserved, always thinking and evaluating what is being said and working out the most logical response. You will hear them say things like, 'One has to observe carefully the predicament', 'One can accept that there is due cause for actors in the system to respond to differing degrees', etc.

Perspective:	Ultra reasonable.
Feeling Evoked in Others:	Envy.
Intention:	Join me.
Body Language:	Head level, eyebrows normal, body position square on, while leaning slightly back. Arms folded with one hand supporting the chin.

The Distractor

Distractors pretend that there is no problem. They release tension by laughing and joking in the hope that by ignoring the threat it will actually disappear. They are easily confused and often go off in a spin. Their behaviour tends to be erratic and they often appear to be clutching at straws. They fumble and mumble. You'll hear them say things like, 'What if ... maybe we could ... you know', 'Possibly ... well, I suppose not ... but ... '

Perspective:	Disconnected.
Feeling Evoked in Others:	A longing for fun.
Intention:	Tolerate me.
Body language:	Jerky, unsettled, constantly moving and shifting, occasionally flashing a smile (which is immediately followed by a frown and then another smile). Distractors can exhibit the behaviour of all of the other responders: Placater, Blamer, etc.

The Leveller

Levellers are open, calm, confident and rational. They say it as it is and are comfortable being honest and expressing their concerns and feelings. They accept that in life there are challenging times and there can be tension, difference and conflicting positions; and they are happy to engage and connect with them. They go for a win-win position and are happy to compromise if it is beneficial to all parties. You'll hear them say things like, 'Let's do this!' *Levellers are extraordinary people.* They are the true peacemakers of society. They are the Nelson Mandelas of this world.

Perspective:	Mutual respect and co-operation.
Feeling Evoked in Others:	Acceptance.
Intention:	Win-win.
Body Language:	Head upright, palms open, eye contact regular, body squared and facing forward, movements relaxed and comfortable.

Pattern Interrupt

The position best equipped to deal with all the other positions is that of the Leveller. If you want to become an extraordinary relationship-builder, you need to assume that role. Earlier, we looked at the importance of *mirroring* in order to be able to *pace and lead* someone into a certain emotional state. However, mirroring a person who is under major stress is not always appropriate. For example, if I had mirrored the angry youth I encountered, I would've squared up to him, snarled, growled and screamed. My guess is that the outcome would have been *very* different. So, if the person you encounter is already in *blame* mode, mirroring his finger-pointing won't get you very far. There are times when you have to try another approach first.

Sometimes the best approach is to *interrupt* the other person mid-flow. This causes the person some temporary confusion, which gives you the opportunity to take control of the situation. In the world of NLP this is called a Pattern Interrupt. I remember being at a meeting recently where I was pitching for some business. The subject of NLP came up and the client immediately became defensive. He had previously had dealings with an unscrupulous chap who claimed that the client needed NLP in order to 'fix' him. Basically, this guy was out for himself; he was not taking care of his client, so they had a bad experience. During the meeting, I could've gone on the defensive and explained that not all NLP is the same and not every practitioner is the same. Instead, I decided to use a Pattern Interrupt to help get us back on track. So I looked at my watch and said, 'I can appreciate that you are a busy man and I won't take up too much more of your time but one of the things I want to discuss with you before I go is your website.' This immediately startled the client because discussion of his website was outside the remit of my proposal. This drew his attention away from his negative experience of the other 'NLP guy'. I offered the client a few tips that he could use immediately: I showed him how making simple alterations to his website could increase his business. In doing this, I took charge of the situation again. From here, I led the conversation back on track and brought it to a successful conclusion. I managed to get the business I was pitching for *and* keep the client happy at the same time. Weeks later, I told the client what I had done. He shrugged, laughed and said, 'I'm glad you did that because you were very nearly *not* getting the business because of my experience with the last guy!' Since that first meeting, the client and I have done a substantial amount of work together. The website advice that he got for free has produced a big increase in his business – and it didn't cost him a cent to implement. I'm convinced that when you do things with the right *intentions*, they work out fine. I took a gamble by offering him free advice and by distracting him in that way. In distracting him, the intention was not to manipulate him or to pull the wool over his eyes. I simply wanted to secure his co-operation for a mutually beneficial contract and, in the end, it worked out very well for both of us. Building relationships in this way is vital to creating an extraordinary life.

CHAPTER 5

Body Talk

I speak two languages: Body and English.
Mae West

S he sat directly across from me, at a distance of around twenty feet, silently listening, observing and absorbing. She was slim and tall. Her blue eyes were gentle and her lips were sealed. Her black hair was shoulder-length, with soft waves running through it. She wore a light woollen top with pink and white patterning. Her long, fauve skirt rested softly against her legs and appeared to float whenever she moved. Her clothes looked new but they weren't fashionable. She had a style all her own: earthy and feminine with a degree of sophistication. I knew she was the one …

It is a month later and I am in her home. I am sitting down and my eyes are closed. My head is tilted downwards and my body is slumped. I don't think I could sink any deeper inside myself if I tried. It is as if my thoughts have become unhinged; they surface spontaneously from the abyss. There is no stopping now. There is no turning back. My stomach is churning and my emotions are building. There is so much I want to say. Inside, it feels like a storm is brewing but every time I try to speak, my tone is subdued and all I can do is mumble.

She stares at me and suddenly the fight is on. *Do I or don't I? Will I or won't I? Is this what I have chosen? Really? In a year's time, I'll be alive as long as Jesus was – and look what happened to him!*

Subconscious memories bubble and flash to the surface with piercing emotion. The words cascade like lava from my mouth. My mind is on fire. My senses are ignited. Images surface from every direction and time space. Without discrimination, the past, present and future merge to make meaning.

She is present; I can feel that. How will she deal with all of this? How will I deal with it? This is not an easy process. It's going to be tough but I have to see it through. I know I will survive. They can't lock me up. Sure,

I'm angry right now but I know I'm not a bad person.

I can't do this! How can you say that? I just can't do this! In a flash, I see myself approaching the door to her home ... Then I see myself as a teenager, wearing my Doc Martens and combats ... Now I'm in a barn, practising with my old band ... Now I see myself being born. I'm at home. I can see the bed. There is a silhouette at a distance. It is staring at me, empathising but not interfering ...

Now my eyes open and I look in the direction of my hypnotherapist. She looks subdued and full of doubt. After a long time, she speaks but it's clear she doesn't understand. She just doesn't understand. And I can't understand what she's saying to me, either. We both speak but there is just so much misunderstanding. There is so much left unsaid. There we are: two people in this intense situation that neither of us can understand ...

There have been so many times in my life when something happens and the human response that I witness is a confusing mystery to me. Certain things just don't add up. Words say one thing; the face that says the words contradicts them entirely. A body suggests one thing and an action contradicts it completely. From the beginning, we are all conditioned to act in certain ways. We are taught to mask emotions, conceal gestures and speak when spoken to. *Don't say such and such – not when such and such is around. Sit up straight. Stop picking your nose! Put that down. Stop moving about.* The list goes on and on. Our natural expressions end up being caged and, before we know it, we become unintentional agents of deception.

This chapter is designed to help you make sense of the things that we don't say with words but with our *bodies*. My hope for you is that by the end of it you will have all the tools you need to make extraordinary leaps in your ability to communicate at a significant and influential level. Think about the difference it would make to your life if you knew what to do for your partner *before* you are asked. How good would it feel to know that you could stop an argument before it started or appease a person before they got too stressed? Imagine being able reach beyond words to affect another person. The tools you learn in this chapter will bring your communication to a brand new level of sophistication and finesse.

A Few Golden Rules

According to a study carried out in 2001, the human body is capable of making 700,000 movements. We won't cover all of them in this chapter! It is enough to say that body language affects us all and we are all experts in it to some degree. It is something you have being studying since you were born.

One of the things to keep in mind when it comes to studying body language in a more formal way is *context*. The same gesture expressed in different situations can mean very different things. Switch on the TV and you're likely to see a politician being interviewed or giving a speech. Notice how they dramatise certain gestures in an attempt to send out their message. They often make expansive movements; keeping their arms at a slight distance from their bodies gives them a stronger presence and makes them look more powerful. Sometimes they'll smile without raising their eyebrows. In isolation, these gestures can be taken lightly; but clusters of gestures can be very powerful and very revealing for the acute observer.

What's it All About Anyway?

What's body language all about? In a nutshell, it's about *feelings*. What the body tells us is what the body is feeling. Words are often used to distract us from what's going on; and they work well. We ask how someone is and they say, 'Great – not a bother!' Often, their body language reveals a different story. Hiding the truth with words is one thing; hiding the truth with our body language is very difficult. Our bodies are more powerful than our words and we have far less control over them. When we try to hide the truth, we use *masking gestures* and we end up with *leakage* or *tells*. It's a bit like holding water in your hands: when you focus on keeping in the water in one area, it often leaks out in a different area.

Even though we can try to hide our feelings, they are actually hardwired into our *faces*. They are genetically programmed and the expressions they give rise to are universal. They are what psychologists refer to as the basic emotions: joy, sorrow, fear, disgust, surprise and anger. It is little wonder then that when we experience the power of these genetically-coded feelings, it is very difficult for us not to reveal them in our gestures.

The Core Patterns

When trying to interpret body language it is important to see it in context. In this way you will notice the dynamics between people in communication. You may see two people in a conversation that becomes animated: one person leans in close, while the other person leans right back. You might have no idea what words are being said, but it is plain to see that one person is happy and the other person is not. These *macro gestures* can be observed from afar and they can be surprisingly accurate. If you master reading these macro gestures, you can later fine-tune your skills and learn about the micro gestures. In all communication, there are *core patterns* that recur and are easily identifiable.

Watch This Space

People often say things like, 'Get out of my face.' They use phrases like this when their personal boundaries have been crossed without their permission. I had an issue with this recently when we got our new kitchen installed. The project manager involved was short-sighted and not very socially aware. The result being that, whenever he chose to talk to me, he would nearly step on my toes because he was so close. He wore glasses and because he came in so close, all I could focus on was the magnifying effect of his glasses. They seemed to make his eyes look huge and the whole thing was very unsettling! I quickly learned a few tricks to keep him at a distance. I avoided standing with my back to a wall. I kept a physical barrier in place any time I could: before I'd ask him a question, I'd grab a chair or something and put it in front of me so he couldn't step right into my personal space. I was lucky to have my wife Theresa there, too. I'd intentionally provoke questions from her to distract the project manager if he was getting too close. Theresa knew exactly what I was at, of course, and later called in some favours of her own …

I think most of us are aware that there is an amount of space that people feel comfortable having between one another. Each of us surrounds ourselves with invisible personal boundaries; and we each have our own rules for who is allowed pass through. Different boundaries are set for different people and situations. The safer we feel, the closer we allow the person to be. There is an area of scientific study on this, called *proxemics*. Scientists suggest that we have five separate zones with specific measurements. Any breach of the zone causes us to feel uncomfortable or even threatened. It's vital to always remain aware of boundaries by staying alert to the responses of a person when you are in their company.

Zone	Distance	People typically permitted
Close intimate	0–15 cm	Lovers
Intimate	15–45 cm	Really close friends
Personal	45–120 cm	Family and close friends
Social and business	1.2–3.6 m	Colleagues and acquaintances
Public	3.6 m plus	Rest of the world

The Opening Pattern

We open up when we are feeling confident or powerful. We open to receive, engage, listen, flirt, or sometimes to show that we are not afraid or threatened. For example, when two alpha males share the same space, they may use very relaxed body language in order to show how unthreatened they feel in each other's company.

When we trust the people in our surroundings, we open up. We do this by lifting our head from the down position to the forward position. We unfold our arms. We show the palms our hands. We keep our legs slightly separated and our feet angled outwards.

Posture:	Sitting or standing upright.
Head:	Facing forward.
Chin:	Facing forward.
Arms:	Unfolded.
Hands:	Palms up.
Legs:	Uncrossed and spaced slightly apart.
Feet:	Angled outwards.

The Expanding Pattern

We expand when we want to show that we are powerful. Men do it all the time to impress women; and it can also be used aggressively to signal a readiness to attack. Women can also expand to protect their loved ones. We expand when we are filled with pride or when we want people to notice us. For example, a person at a seminar may brace themselves and expand before they speak to the room.

Posture:	Standing (or sitting) as tall as possible.
Head:	Straight.
Chin:	Jutting forward.
Nose:	Nostrils flared.
Chest:	Puffed outwards.
Arms:	Extended and suspended alongside body.
Hands:	Opened and widened.
Legs:	Standing in the 'A' position.
Feet:	Facing forward.

The Protective Pattern

If we are uncomfortable or under threat, we are likely to try to protect ourselves. We do this by covering our exposed areas. We fold our arms. We hold our hands. We intertwine our fingers. We cross our legs.

Arms:	Folded.
Hands:	Held together.
Fingers:	Intertwined.
Legs:	Crossed.
Feet:	Ankles crossed.

The Retreat Pattern

Sometimes when we are in the presence of someone that we feel is more powerful than us, we react by retreating; rather than leaving their company altogether, we pull back physically. Often, we will retreat if do not like the other person being in our space. This doesn't always mean that we don't actually like the person, but they may have something about them that we find off-putting, e.g. bad breath. When we retreat, we can lean back or turn away altogether. We may pull our head back while dipping our chin, covering our exposed throat, if we feel threatened. The retreat pattern is sometimes used as a flirting gesture: one partner steps back as a test to see if the other partner moves in to fill the space.

Posture:	Leaning back.
Head:	Pulled back or turned away.
Chin:	Dipped, to cover throat.
Chest:	Pulled back and inwards.
Arms:	Pulled back.
Legs:	Stepping back.
Feet:	Stepping back.

The Advance Pattern

Sometimes we advance as an act of aggression, to signal our anger or upset. This gesture happens quickly and is used to ward off the other person. We can also advance when we want to show that we are interested in another person, perhaps romantically. This gesture happens gradually and is tempered by the response of the other person.

Posture:	Leaning forward.
Head:	Pushed forward.
Chin:	Facing forward.
Chest:	Leaning forward.
Arms:	Touching, giving, grabbing, striking.
Hips:	Thrust forward.
Legs:	Moving forward.
Feet:	Stepping forward.

Self-Soothing Patterns

When we feel threatened, uncertain, stressed, uncomfortable or excited, we are likely to engage in self-soothing patterns. The patterns are easily identifiable because they involve self-directed touch. The purpose of the touch is to reassure or affirm ourselves. We soothe ourselves when we lie. We soothe ourselves when we are physically stressed. We also do it when we are interested in someone: by rubbing or touching the area that we would like *them* to touch.

Posture:	Varies.
Hair:	Stroking or flicking – flirting.
Forehead:	Palm to forehead – something bad happens, you make a mistake or do something stupid.
Neck:	Rubbing the back of neck – discomfort.
Eyes:	Rubbing or blocking the eyes – avoid seeing something; signalling that you want to be elsewhere.
Nose:	Rubbing the nose – disagreement or discomfort. Pinching the bridge in – feeling critical. Fingering – thinking. Scratching – lying. Touching the side – signalling a secret.
Mouth:	Covering with the hand – signalling the desire to stay silent. Hands to mouth – shocked or stuck for words.
Lips:	Finger to lips – signalling silence.
Teeth:	Tapping the teeth – bored or annoyed.
Chin:	Stroking the chin – thinking.
Cheek:	Hands cradling cheeks – horror.
Chest:	Rubbing – tense.
Stomach:	Rubbing – tense, full or hungry.
Arms:	Rubbing or stroking – need comforting or warmth.
Hands:	Cupping, rubbing, clasping – comfort or signalling readiness for action.
Hips:	Caressing hips, bottom, legs or thighs – desire.

Attraction Patterns

When it comes to attraction, men and women have some patterns in common and some that are gender specific. Here are some of the patterns common to both men and women.

Making Eye Contact

A man will scan and stare, whereas a woman will be more subtle. When a man or woman is interested, they will seek eye contact and then hold the stare a little longer than normal. A woman will typically look away, possibly downwards. She will look back up, then away again a number of times. She may flicker her eyelashes and lengthen the duration of the stare. The eyes of both the man and the woman will moisten. They will look smitten – and this is generally known as a 'lovers' gaze'. A man and woman can also signal interest with a gentle 'yes' nod of the head when eye contact is made. They will both smile but a woman will smile more often. The direction of the eyes can be revealing: looking at the lips may be an indication that a man or woman wants to kiss. The pupils of the eyes naturally dilate for a man and a woman who are interested in each other. It is as if they can't see enough of each other.

Beautifying

Preening is the act of making oneself look more attractive to another person. A man will preen by expanding his chest and arms to make them look bigger and stand out from the crowd. A woman will preen by flicking her hair, fixing her clothes or polishing her glasses.

Displaying

A man and a woman will push out their chests and hold in their tummies in order to appear more attractive. Women will sway their hips or reveal their legs, while men may reveal their torso or arms. Sometimes men will assume the 'cowboy stance', putting their hands in their pockets with their thumbs pointing in the direction of their private parts. Women will show interest by exposing their vulnerable areas: the neck, inner wrists or forearms. Dancing is often used as a means of looking more sensual and appealing.

Acting Out

Rubbing the thighs, calves, hips, bottom, arms or face can be an unconscious expression of the desire to be touched in the same way by another person. Women will often lick their lips when interested romantically. Stroking the stem of a wine glass, playing with a pen, slipping a ring or shoe on and off again are all enactment signals.

Body Direction

A person will often signal interest by pointing in the direction of the another person. This may be face forward to get full visual contact or it may be done more subtly, by pointing feet, knees or arms in the direction of the other person.

Leaning Forward

Leaning forward into a person's space is a way of showing interest. This can also be shown by standing closer than normal to the person and paying close attention to what they are saying. A natural rapport can develop, which produces mirroring and matching gestures.

Physical Contact

This can start accidentally-on-purpose: one person brushing up against another in passing. It can then move to more obvious gestures: gentle, occasional touching of acceptable parts of the body, such as the arms or back. This in turn can progress into more intimate touching, if the advances are welcomed. Removing fluff from a person's clothing is also an enactment signal.

Standing Up and Stepping Out

When you choose to follow your own path, there will be people who do not take kindly to your standing up and stepping out. It is not unusual for the people around you to want you to remain as you are and not change. This way, they can understand you or perhaps even *control* you. There may be occasions when you are faced with the challenge of dealing with someone who acts contrary to your needs and goals. It is unlikely that you will have to deal with very extreme forms of resistance, such as aggression, but it is no harm to be able to handle it if it ever comes up.

How to Tell If Someone is Becoming Physically Aggressive

In Chapter 1, we saw that the first *need* on the Wheel of Human Potential is *safety*. In psychologically healthy people, any perceived threat to their personal safety automatically consumes their attention. That is not to say that we never take risks with our safety, e.g. driving at high speed. There is evidence everywhere of people actually taking risks with their lives: jumping from incredible heights, etc. We may call these people reckless or even mad for dicing with death, but in general you'll find that they take these risks in full knowledge of what they are doing. They are acutely aware of the implications for their safety; human beings generally are. This is why we are actually quite good at spotting the signs of aggression in other people.

Most aggression becomes immediately obvious through facial expressions. The aggressor frowns, stares, flares their nostrils and purses their lips. If they are getting ready to attack, they clench their fists, fix their feet firmly on the ground and expand their body. Their muscles become taut and tense. Their face reddens as their heart rate speeds up. If they are preparing to strike, they may look away or turn away briefly before initiating the blow. If they are confident in their aggression, they may offer an 'invitation'. (Remember 'Are you gonna call the bleedin' coppers?' in Chapter 4?) This is to express dominance by *daring* the person to challenge them.

The aggressor will invade your personal space and may even make 'fake friendly' gestures, e.g. the mafia 'kiss of death'. This is intended to cause confusion: it distracts and disarms the intended target, as they try to figure out whether the gesture is sincere or not. It's not unusual for the aggressor to touch the person and bring them into their own personal space with a hug or a slap on the back. The giveaway can be that bit of added *force* in the hug or squeeze.

Sometimes you will get a bit of enactment or acting out – all of it done in an apparently joking manner. The aggressor may take a false swing or make a series of air punches, while appearing to be happy, laughing and making jokes. In extreme forms of aggression, there may be *flash gestures* in an attempt to shock or surprise.

In less threatening situations, the aggressor may displace their anger onto objects: hitting, punching or slapping a wall or door forcefully. Sometimes they will throw objects at or around their target. Think of those stock movie scenes where a person thrashes their surroundings because they lose control of their temper. What they are saying here is that they would like to do that to a *person*. You must never be around a person when they are in this state. Your best move is to head for the nearest door and get away from it all.

How to Deal With Physical Aggression or Anger

1. If you can get out, do. Leave the aggressor to blow off steam and give them the space to cool down. This is *their* problem, not yours, even if it is directed at you. It is how they are choosing to respond to it.

2. Avoid reasoning with them: it won't work. They are not thinking reasonably so they will not respond reasonably.

3. The level of anger will determine your response. If they are likely to become violent and you can't get out, then remain silent. Try to avoid expressing strong emotion, such as anger, fear or sorrow; this will just attract attention. If the aggressor's behaviour is not typical and is unlikely to be violent, then remain quiet and ignore the behaviour. The behaviour is intended to *get a response* from you. If you do not respond, the aggressor will have to try something else to get your attention. Your aim is to avoid engagement of any kind, verbal or gestural. Basically, *shut down* on the inside and become unemotional. Do not offer any responses whatsoever: no expressions of disdain, no sighs of exasperation, no signals of disappointment, nothing. *Just shut down.* Be aware, though, that the aggressor may escalate the behaviour in order to get you to react. Again, if you can't get away, just remain silent and unemotional.

4. There can be extreme situations of aggression and anger, but there can also be milder ones. If a person begins having an angry episode that seems out of character for them, stop them and say, 'Not *this* way … I am walking away now but I will talk to you when you have had time to cool down.' It might take a while for the pressure to lift, but when it does, follow through with your offer to communicate. Wait for the person to be in a good mood or set up a pleasant atmosphere that promotes dialogue. If you can, have the chat in a neutral place, different from where the anger occurred. Tell the person that you want to work out what caused the upset.

5. Focus on the issue, not on the behaviour. If the anger starts to return, repeat your objective clearly. Do this in a slightly softer tone than normal, without recrimination or blame.

6. If the person doesn't meet you half way, get up and leave.

7. If they fail to come to reason themselves or open a dialogue with you afterwards, you need to make up your own mind about your own position on the matter and stick with that.

Most of us have the good fortune not to have to deal with situations of extreme aggression or anger. The following scenarios are much more common.

How to Tell If Someone is Trying to Overpower You Without Physical Violence

Trying to dominate someone is a form of aggression but it can be subtle. An aggressor in this context will make their body bigger and sit or stand taller. They will invade your personal space. Did you ever notice on *X Factor* that Simon Cowell used to place his hand on the back of Cheryl Cole's chair? I always saw that as a deliberate attempt at dominance. Such attempts usually confuse or upset the person to the extent that they cannot think clearly. Displays of dominance usually involve the breaking of social etiquette and they are an attempt to show the world 'who is boss'.

People can use other symbols or signals in an attempt to express dominance. This can be done with property or things: driving the most expensive car, owning the largest office or wearing the most expensive jewellery. The crucial thing here is that *owning* the thing is not enough: people want to assert authority by *flaunting* these things. So, showing off a fancy new office or shiny new car can be an attempt at gaining power.

Any form of invasion into another person's *space* is an attempt to dominate. The man who sits on a lady's chair when she gets up to talk to someone; the woman who is over-friendly with her friend's husband; the office worker who puts his feet up on a colleague's desk; the colleague who is over-friendly and insincere; all of these people are trying to claim power. They are saying that they can do what they like, and they can take what they like.

How a person behaves in a *shared space* will say a lot about them. If a person stands directly in your way or in your line of sight, while having their back to you, that is an expression of dominance. Walking towards you and refusing to step aside even though there is room for two on the pathway, is another telling behaviour. These are all acts of aggression intended to assert dominance. The basic message here is: 'I am important and you are not.'

Dominance can be asserted by sneering at a person or ignoring them when they speak. A stronger form occurs if the aggressor deliberately checks their nails or looks away in an overtly uninterested manner. Some men engage in very crass dominance behaviours when another person tries to speak. They may spread their legs wide and even scratch themselves inappropriately, the message being: 'Mine is bigger than yours.' Some aggressors insist on speaking before everyone else and in a louder tone of voice. Interrupting people can be another attempt at dominance. Have you ever noticed that politicians sometimes reach over and place their hand on an opponent's forearm in the middle of a TV debate? This is a prime example of an attempt to dominate and silence another person.

How to Deal With Dominance

One of the most powerful ways to disarm an aggressor is to bring attention to what they are doing: 'Excuse me. I do not appreciate you standing in front of me and blocking my view.' Stating exactly what is happening is another powerful tool: 'Your behaviour is aggressive.'

Provided there is no threat of physical danger, you could always play aggressors at their own game. So, if they lock on and stare, you do the same. If they interrupt your conversation, you speed up your own speech, increase your volume and tell them unequivocally and in a firm tone of voice to let you finish. If they invade your space and touch you, you touch them back. If they try to overpower you with a 'hand on top' handshake, reach out and hold their elbow, then step to the side.

Handshakes and other welcome greetings can be very revealing. There are some amusing videos on YouTube, showing interactions between politicians and the dominant body language that so often accompanies these encounters. Politicians are very aware of body language and of the power of symbolism, so when the cameras roll, they take their opportunity. Frequently, you'll see the leader of one country stepping back to welcome the leader of another. In doing so, they gently tap the back of the other politician, as if to say, 'You're ok, little man; I'll look after you.'

Telling Lies

There are times when it will be really important to know if someone is telling you the truth or not. Researchers tell us that the average person is *lied to* nearly 200 hundred times a day! Being lied to can leave a person feeling vulnerable, stupid, dejected and angry; but it happens to each of us at some point. It's fair to say that most lies we are told are fibs or white lies and sometimes that's ok. Your girlfriend says, 'Do I look fat in this?' If you want the relationship to continue, the right answer is always *no*, even if the truth is different. So little white lies are harmless enough but there is a darker side to human behaviour and sometimes a person lies not to protect your feelings, but out of malice.

Did you know?
Here's an interesting rule of thumb. When a person who is telling the truth is challenged, they will go on the *offensive*. When a person who is telling a lie is challenged, they will go on the *defensive*.

When people lie, they like to justify their behaviour. The trap they often fall into is that they actually don't buy their own press. Their justifications don't stand up and they know this, so they end up feeling tense. *Tension* gets reflected in the body through jerky or twitchy movements. You may hear a clearing of the throat as the person begins to speak. This may be combined with a twitching, touching or flickering of the eyes. Because of the amount of internal energy it takes to lie, the person's natural flow goes off-kilter and they may behave in a clumsy fashion. It is not unusual to notice pauses and hesitation in their language, as they try to think ahead.

Sometimes, in an effort to regain control, the person telling the lie may try to *freeze* some of their gestures. They may try to hold still, hold their arms in a self-soothing gesture or put their hands in their pockets to avoid fidgeting. People who lie a lot do not avoid eye contact: as a matter of fact, they look at you closely to observe your response, so that they can find out if the lie is working or not. Inexperienced 'liars' will try and change the subject quickly; more experienced liars will have rehearsed their story so much that they may even enjoy trying it out on you.

Silence causes tension in the liar so they often fill the space with words. If your friend gives an unusually long-winded explanation for why they couldn't meet you some night, they might be lying. If you hear a story like the one below, chances are your friend is telling fibs.

> Wait until I tell you what happened last night! Well, you know Dana from school? I hadn't seen her in ages and I decided to ring her out of the blue and, well, her brother's dog – he is a little black and white Yorkshire terrier – got knocked down at about quarter past six last night and she was really upset. She was crying and sobbing on the phone and all. She was only after buying the little dog one of those sparkly collars – you know the ones that you get down in Tesco? Anyway, *that's* why I didn't make it to the party. Really sorry about that ... Do you want to go out Friday instead?

The basic intent behind lying is to avoid getting caught and the natural impulse response to this is to get out of the situation as soon as possible. This urge to avoid the pressure of scrutiny leaks into the words the liar speaks. They'll try to disassociate themselves from their own actions.

Evidence of lying can be seen on a person's face, through their *microexpressions*. Microexpressions are the expressions that flash in a person's face and then disappear quickly. When a person lies, they often try to force a smile or fake friendliness. They may scratch their face or nose and cover their mouth. Their vocal chords may tense, which causes their voice to change and move to a higher pitch.

Remember that people can make these gestures for *other* reasons, so keep context in mind and pay attention to clusters of gestures. If you suspect someone of lying, it's good to establish a baseline for their behaviour. If you can, find out how they behave when they are *not* lying and measure that against what happens when you think they *are* lying. If they are lying, they will switch between the baseline and another set of behaviours a number of times while spinning their yarn.

Sometimes there are no obvious *physical* indicators that a person is lying. If that is the case, there are usually other detectors in their language.

How to Spot Someone Who is Telling Lies

1. As Judge Judy says: 'If it doesn't make sense, then it is not true!' Always apply *logic* to what 'the liar' is telling you. Examine their story and ask yourself if the facts stack up. If you suspect deception, ask the person to tell you the run of events in reverse order, i.e. tell the story backwards. If they are lying, they won't be able to do it; if they are telling the truth, they will.

2. If a person is recounting an event truthfully, they will use a lot of 'I' in their story. For example:

   > It must have been around ten o'clock because the neighbours had their bins out. The first thing I did was switch on the lights and then I saw that the bedroom door was open and I saw a knife on the floor with blood on it and so I immediately thought something was after happening to Jane.

   If a person is telling lies, they will try to disassociate themselves from the story. Notice how 'the liar' tells this same story in much greater detail. Crucially, the word 'I' has been left out for the most part.

   > It is 10 pm, I am coming up the driveway and the house is in darkness. Once the lights are switched on, it is obvious that someone has been in the house. The bedroom door is partially opened and there is a blood-stained knife on the floor, to the right of the locker by the bed. The thought immediately strikes me that something dreadful has happened to Jane.

3. People telling the truth usually use the appropriate tense.

Reread the examples above and notice how the person telling the truth uses the past tense (since the action happened in the past) but the person telling lies uses the present tense. Pay attention to the tense used by a person you suspect is lying to you.

4. People who are lying often answer a question by repeating the question in their own answer.

> Did you put a knife to Jane Doe and cut her throat and let her bleed to death?

> Do I look like the kind of person that would put a knife to someone's throat and let them bleed to death?

5. People who are lying use *modifiers* when asked questions. This is a form of hedging and avoidance.

> Is it fair to say that you were in the house at the time?

> Well I **guess** you could say that, **maybe;** but it **probably** isn't **really** an accurate statement. But I don't know: you're the expert, **aren't you?** What in your opinion do you think could have **possibly** happened?

Words like 'believe', 'guess', 'suppose', 'maybe' and 'possibly' are all words that *modify* the statements made and leave them open to questioning. That is exactly what the liar wants: deflection.

6. People who are lying often over-emphasise and try and add weight to their lies by saying things like: 'I swear', 'on my honour', 'cross my heart' or 'as God is my witness'.

7. People who are lying leave out insignificant details that people who tell the truth usually include. In the example above, the person telling the truth mentioned his neighbours' bins.

Former US President Bill Clinton told a famous lie: 'I did not have sexual relations with that woman.' Notice the *distancing*: the personal secretary he had known for years was referred to as 'that woman'. Notice, too, how the sex act is *modified*: 'sexual relations' sounds more impersonal. The use of the formal negative is also curious: 'I did **not** have'. It would be more usual to say 'I *didn't* have'.

Exercise: Try Out Your New Skills

Ask your friend to make up a story that is a lie and tell them to mix it amongst some other stories that are true. Make sure they give you enough detail to be able to work with: each story should have at least five or six sentences. Use the following tips to figure out which story is untrue:

1. Establish your baseline behaviour.
2. Pay attention to the logic and sequence. Does it add up?
3. Look out for the presence (or absence) of 'I'.
4. What tense is used?
5. When you ask them a question, do they answer you with the question?
6. Do they offer many 'oaths'?
7. Do they stick to the answer or are there insignificant details included?
8. What about their use of negation?
9. What is their body doing?
10. What does their body language say to you?

Develop Your Skills

The topics covered in this chapter are by no means exhaustive, but you should now have the ability to read the signals that people are sending out during your interactions with them. This will give you the opportunity to stay ahead of the game. I suggest that you explore these skills in a safe environment first, e.g. with your partner or family. Spend some time using your rapport-building skills to see if you can pace and lead people into more resourceful states.

You can also learn a lot by watching TV shows that involve debate of some kind. I think Vincent Browne is a provocative presenter with a superb intellect and a fine sense of humour. He puts these skills to great use in getting past the masks and defences used by his interviewees, who are generally politicians. Watch his show (or similar ones) and you will see composure and its subsequent decomposition under duress. You will see territorial displays, expansive gestures and dominance patterns. There is an entire world to be explored by observing these interactions.

In Chapter 6, we will move beyond the body and return to studying the mind. We will explore how psychological preferences determine how you are motivated, how you make decisions, how you sort for information and how you perform a whole range of other tasks. We will examine human personalities and learn how to predict what other people think.

Going Mental

I must have a prodigious amount of mind;
it takes me as much as a week, sometimes, to make it up!
Mark Twain

Sensory Preference

In Chapters 3 and 4 we identified that people develop certain sensory preferences in life. People place an emphasis on how things *look*, how things *sound*, or how things *feel*. A smaller number of people have a preference for *taste and smell*. We have seen that we can identify sensory preferences by observing how a person uses language. This gives us an indication of how to interact with them on the level at which they are most comfortable.

When a person displays a preference for *sight*, we know that if we want to connect with them on a meaningful level, we ought to give them visual explanations. If we are presenting to them, we could use diagrams or pictures, photos or any other type of visual media. If we are teaching them to do something, the quickest way will be to show them how to do it – either by doing it ourselves or by letting them see someone else do it.

When a person displays a preference for *sound*, speaking to them is going to be important. If you want to sell them an idea or get them to do something, sending them an e-mail will be far less effective than picking up the phone and talking to them. Having a chat face to face will be most effective. If they are coming to your office for a meeting that you suspect might be challenging, play some relaxing music in the waiting room – it is sure to help.

If *touch* is the sensory preference of a person, they will respond well to a hug or a handshake. They will be interested in atmospheres and comfort. So taking your time, slowing down your speech and giving them room to process their thoughts will be very much appreciated by them. If you want them to do something, it is best that they do it as you guide them through the process; they learn best through experience. If you want to sell them a car, give them a test drive. If you want to sell them a holiday, explore how they will *feel* if they go on this trip. Talk with them about the places they will visit and the things they will do there. Take them on an emotional journey; and give them time to build the feelings and the desire to want to go there.

Exercise: Identify Your Sensory Preference

In the box below, write a description of how you spent your day yesterday. Then read over your text and pay attention to the language that you used. Which sensory preference did you rely on most?

Yesterday I spent my day...
_____
_____
_____
_____
_____
_____
_____

Meta Programs

Knowledge of a person's sensory preference allows you to partially predict their likely choices. However, there are other operations going on that affect and influence how a person will respond to inputs. It is clear that there are other levels of cognition at which behaviour is relatively stable and predictable. As human beings, we engage in a psychological *sorting process* as we make sense of the world around us. This process reflects preferences that we develop in certain contexts. In NLP, this sorting process is defined as our use of Meta Programs. Meta Programs are programs that guide and direct other thought processes. They focus less on the *content* of incoming information or input and more on the *organisation* of it.

In the same way that we can be selective about how we attend to sensory data, we can also be selective about how we operate our Meta Programs. There are a number of these programs or patterns and we will explore the most common ones below. The programs can work simultaneously and they can adjust and change according to context, so a pattern in one setting may shift to its exact opposite in another setting. It is important to keep in mind two key words as we go along: *preference* and *context*. These two words point to the fact that you have the ability to change your preference according to your needs.

If you like the idea of being extraordinary, then there is a huge opportunity in learning about Meta Programs. I suggest that you first identify the programs that you use most often; and then, like a method actor preparing for a role, experiment with other programs. Play around with them and see what they feel like. When you do, your life experience will increase dramatically and you will be truly capable of extraordinary feats.

The Primary Interest Pattern: Which Do You Prefer?

Have you ever noticed that there are certain people you meet and you 'hit it off with them' straight away? This usually comes down to common interests. Overall, our interests can be divided into five categories: people, places, things, activities and information.

People

A person with a primary interest in people focuses on the *who* in any interaction. If you ask them what they are doing for the weekend, they will usually talk about the *people* they will be with. They will often start their sentences with 'we':

> We've decided to take it easy this weekend. We'll probably sit and watch a DVD or something. I am expecting the brother and his wife to drop in and we'll probably just have a bit of a laugh, you know, a few beers maybe.

Notice how this person highlights their experience by talking about the people involved. A people-focused person enjoys the company of other people. They enjoy being around them, talking with them and getting to know them. If you tell them a story, they'll be sure to ask you who was there, what they were like, whether you met anyone new, etc.

Places

A person with a primary interest in places focuses on the *where* in any interaction. If you ask them what they are doing for the weekend, they will usually talk about the places they will go to. They will focus on location:

> I'm going down to Casey's pub on Bridge Street for a few pints and I might drop into O'Neills across the way for a few more before I head to the chippers for the usual. Not that chippers on Sandyford Avenue, now – the one across from the park, just off Ferills Road. You know where they're after building that new shopping complex at the junction of Newlands Cresent? That one there.

Notice how this person highlights their experience by talking about the places involved.

People and places are the most frequent patterns. Often, a person will demonstrate a preference for both, with one just a little stronger than the other. This will be obvious if you examine their speech preferences.

Things

A person with a primary interest in things focuses on the *what* in any interaction. They are interested in objects. If you ask them what they are doing for the weekend, they will usually talk about the things involved:

> I'm heading up to Woodies DIY. There's this new, state of the art hammer action drill that I've had my eye on for a while. If I can get that, then I'll have the full set.

Notice how this person focuses on the things involved. These people are the collectors and, in extreme cases, can be hoarders. Think of the person with a garage full of gadgets and objects: this is a person who feels good owning or having things. They like to have 'stuff' and it's not always based on need; sometimes it's about want. 'I don't like going away because I like to have my own things around me; it just feels right, you know, homely.'

If you ask them where they have been, they will focus on *what* was there. If they went to a restaurant, they'll tell you what they had to eat, whether they got a deal or not, and what the tables, chairs, windows, doors and floors looked like (whether you want this detail or not).

Activities

A person with a primary interest in activities focuses on the *how* in any interaction. They love to know how stuff works. They always ask, 'How did you do that?' If you ask them what they are doing for the weekend, they will usually talk about the events and activities involved:

> I'm going to Liberty Hall. There's a protest on and I want to be in it. You should come in: there's going to a big bash afterwards in Stephen's Green. Today FM will be there and I think there will be a few live bands playing. Did I tell you I'm heading off on Sunday to do some camping, too? I might do a bit of mountain climbing or maybe I'll take the bike and bring it for a spin.

These people are all about the activities. They are the guys with the ants in their pants! They are always on the go. If you show them something you have just bought, they will pick it up, examine it and want to figure out how it works.

Information

A person with a primary interest in information has lots of questions about any interaction! They want to know *who, what, when, where, why* and *how*. They love to learn and they love gathering facts and figures. They thrive on information: the more detail you give them, the happier they are.

If you ask them what they are doing for the weekend be prepared, be very prepared. They will tell you about it and they will leave no stone unturned. If you want to keep them busy, give them the instruction manual for your fridge and ask them if they've read it. If they haven't done so already, they will now; and it'll keep them intrigued for hours. While they have an insatiable appetite for information, they usually don't bother with gossip. They are more interested in any information that adds to their knowledge.

> Did you notice how I gave the information-focused people (above) a bit of a hard time? As you learn about Primary Interest Patterns, you'll notice that we often try to impose our own preferences on others. Everyone thinks that their own way of doing things is 'normal'.

The Towards/Away From Pattern: Pain or Pleasure?

When you read the title of this book, *From Ordinary to Extraordinary*, what were your initial thoughts? Maybe you thought, 'Extraordinary? Extraordinary? I am already *fantabulous*. What would I want to be extraordinary for?' If that was your thought, thank you so much for buying my humble little book. I hope it can add that extra bit of shine to your sparkle …

Most people do *not* think in this way, though. Their thoughts are more indepth and revealing. They will usually have one dominant thought that says something about their Towards/Away From Pattern. It might be, 'What would this book be able to do for me?' Or it might be, 'This book will help me to solve some issues.' These perspectives come from different angles. While it's possible that you had *both* of these responses, what was your first thought? Which thought triggered the stronger response? The two perspectives are very different. The first perspective involves *looking for what you can get* and the second involves *emphasising what you haven't got yet*.

Everyone has their own approach to problems and goals. Some people immediately focus on what they will get, gain, achieve or be able to do. Theirs is a pull *towards what they want*. Other people immediately focus on the disadvantages, dangers, threats or possible mistakes. Theirs is a pull *away from what they don't want*.

Do you find that your goals and problems pull you towards them? Do you like setting priorities and are you good at managing them? This shows a preference for moving towards pleasure. Do you respond well to incentives, bonuses and rewards? If so, you have a preference for moving towards opportunities. If you are more focused on what can or has to be done, to the extent that you can overlook potential pitfalls or problems, then you have a *moving towards* preference. When considering a new job, do you think about what the perks will be and if it pays well? This is another sign of a preference for moving towards.

When you bought this book, the thoughts that went through your mind revealed a lot about your Towards/Away From Pattern. If you have a preference for *moving towards*, you probably thought:

- Is it any good?
- What will it do for me?
- How will this be of benefit to me?

If you have a preference for *moving away from*, you probably thought:

- Will it be worth the read?
- Do I have the time to read it?
- Is it value for money?
- What problem does this solve?
- Do I really need it?
- If I don't read it, will I be missing out?

If you look closely, you will be able to identify your preference. You might be thinking, 'Ah, no, Brian I didn't give it that much thought at all. I just saw it on the shelf and liked the look of it, so I picked it up and went to the counter.' But that is actually a *moving towards* pattern, when you think about it. You could also say, 'Ah, no, Brian, the book caught my eye and I didn't give it much thought at all, really. I had to get on a plane and I just didn't want to be bored the whole way through the flight.' But that is actually a *moving away from* pattern.

The Proactive/Reactive Pattern: Opportunity or Threat?

People with a preference for moving towards are naturally *proactive*. People with a preference for moving away are naturally *reactive*. If you have a preference for proactivity, you are motivated by doing things. You like to jump in, go to it and get things done. When you are on a roll, the whole world could fall down around you and it wouldn't make a difference: you are on target for your goal and it's going to happen – that's all there is to it! You are the one with ants in your pants, the one who leans forward on the chair and just can't wait to get started. You have to hold off on thinking about your birthday or Christmas too soon for fear that you'll get too excited and won't be able to think about anything else (much like my son). You know the drill: if you fail to plan, you plan to fail. You hate to hear people saying, 'It'll be alright on the night.' None of those shenanigans, thank you! You are easily identifiable by your frequent use of the word 'I'. 'What am I going to do next?' and 'What am I going to do after that?' It's not that it's all about you; you're just in control of your own life. You want to be head honcho in your life – and you should be – so well done.

On the other hand, if you're like me, your thoughts are a little different. It's more like, 'Hang on a minute. Don't be running ahead of yourself, now. Just pause for a moment and catch your breath. We don't have to do everything today all of a sudden and all at once. There is plenty of time to think this through. Let's take a moment before we all end up with egg on our faces!' This shows a preference for *moving away* and a tendency towards being *reactive*. It means that, when faced with an opportunity or threat, you move inwards first and you want to think about it. Sometimes you hesitate and you end up thinking too much. So you can see everything that could go wrong but you can't see what could go right. Sometimes you'll wait years to get the ball rolling: 'Let's wait and see how things pan out first will we?' You sit back in the chair, taking stock of your reaction and everyone else's reaction before you make a move. You weigh up the pros and cons. You are pensive and analytical. You can sit still for ages. When you speak, there are pauses and breaks. Your sentences are full 'aah' and 'hmmm' and 'let me think'. You often feel like you are being pulled around from Billy to Jack. You'll speak about what you *don't* want, rather than what you do want. You seldom use the word 'I'. You prefer to speak of 'it': 'It'll be done ... It'll be alright ... It'll have to wait ... Things are getting on top of me ... Stuff is all over the place!' When you go inside your mind, you are disassociated. You sometimes feel that life is happening *to* you so you are slow to get motivated. However, when you are faced with a problem or threat, you are energised. You are a fixer and an improver. You can't help yourself: 'It just has to be done; you can't just leave it sitting there!' You love to talk about how things might work out. You love if someone asks for your advice on how to fix something. You can be easily distracted, so it's best if you focus on one project at a time. You are a grafter and you work hard. Sometimes you do things at the last minute, though, and this leaves you wide open to stress.

The Power/Connection/Achievement Pattern: Why Bother?

While the presence of opportunities or threats in our world will initially pull us towards or push us away from them, when we do things we need to have *reasons* to do them.

If you like to be in control, if you need to be in control, if you are a control freak, your preference is for *power*. You size up people and situations in terms of who is 'top dog'. You are always the competitive one in the group. You strategise, plan and perhaps even manipulate. You are not afraid of power struggles: in fact, you like nothing better than a good fight. Bring it on! You are energised by resistance and you want to express your power. You like to be able to gauge how well you are doing and you get the greatest kick out of talking about your victories, especially those ones where you pulled yourself from the jaws of defeat in the nick of time. If any of this sounds familiar, you need to get a life. Oops! Sorry, you have a preference for power. I'm not saying you get drunk on the idea or anything but, you know, if the shoe fits ...

What if your preferences are completely different from this? Do you like a good hug? Are you a placator? If so, you have a preference for *connection*. You just love to connect, you love to belong and it's relationships that take priority in your life. You love to include people and you believe that it is very wrong to exclude them. You are the one who walks down the street giving out roses and hugs because you just want everything to be all better. Ok, ok! I'm being a bit cynical here – but you get the gist. You are a people person. You have a strong desire for mutual respect and understanding. You really believe that you ought to treat people the way you would like to be treated yourself. That is because you are a nice person and you judge other people on whether they are nice or not. When you go out, you like to be among your friends. You are the one who will take up the cause of the underdog because there is nothing you hate more than witnessing a person being mistreated.

There is another preference. Sometimes a preference for *achievement* drives a person. If you have this preference, *success* is what excites you. You were born to succeed and *woe betide* anyone who should get in your way! To quote *The Blues Brothers*, you are 'on a mission from God'. Well, God might not have anything to do with it – but you feel very strongly about your mission. For you, it's all about the pursuit of excellence. I have to confess that it's all about the pursuit of excellence for me, too. I understand people who are always striving to improve, to be better and to do better. It's not enough to be ordinary when you could be extraordinary. It's not enough to be happy when you could be ecstatic. If this is your preference, too, you're just a legend of a human being ... Ok, back to earth, Brian! Having a preference for achievement means that you are focused – and quality and standards are important to you. You are able to prioritise and achieve your goals. You think in terms of what you have done and what you have yet to do. Your patience runs low around non-performers or lazy people. You just don't have time for them and you're liable to say, 'Come on! There are things to do, places to go, people to see, you know? Move it along!' You like things to be right. You like things to be at their best. You always try your best to achieve this.

The Time Frame Pattern: How Long Will it Take?

We have preferences in the way we look at *time*. Some people find it quite natural to think well into the future. Some cultures place more emphasis on the past. In Aboriginal cultures, high importance is placed on the long-term past. They suggest that, before you make any decision in life you should go back at least seven generations for advice. Now, I don't even know who my great-grandfather was, never mind being in a position to ask his advice! That's cultural perspective, though. In the West, we often focus on the future. Many cultures of the East focus on the present. Mindfulness, for instance, is all about the value of being in the present moment.

A person's perspective of time will shape their decisions. There are basically three perspectives: past, present and future. If you weigh up your decisions against what you know from experience or how things used to be done, you operate out of the *past*. If you focus on days gone by, enjoy tradition or are particularly averse to change, you have a preference for past. If you have a preference for the *present*, you see no point in crying over spilt milk. You get to the task at hand and you don't worry too much about tomorrow. You are well grounded in the present and you think we should all eat, drink and be merry. You live for the moment. If you find yourself mulling over the consequences of your present actions and thinking about what people will say or do, your focus is on the *future*. You are a particularly good strategist and you feel comfortable working on plans that have not yet been put into action.

There is an added dimension to how a person handles time: it involves whether you think in the short-term, medium-term or long-term. Each perspective offers opportunities and constraints. If you are inclined to think in the short-term, you are likely not to hesitate in making decisions but your lack of foresight could cost you. If you focus on the medium-term, you could come up against unforeseen obstacles that would knock you off track because you weren't thinking long-term enough to make a plan. If you think only in the long-term, you might do so at the expense of enjoying the present moment. You could lose valuable opportunities because of your hesitation to commit until you are satisfied that you have worked out every eventuality.

The Internal/External Reference Pattern: How Are You Doing?

How do you know whether you have done a good job or not on a project or task? What is your first port of call? Do you check *outside* of yourself for feedback? Or do you do an *internal* check to see how you feel about your performance? Now, we all do a bit of both at different times – but again, this is about preferences. If you check in with other people, reports or performance indicators first, your check is obviously external and that is your preference. If you check in with yourself first, then you have a preference for an internal check.

People with an external preference look to others for motivation; and they need feedback to sustain it. It matters to them what other people think. They are often motivated into action by a recommendation: 'If it's good enough for my friend, it's good enough for me.' If you have an internal preference, you will make up your own mind regardless of a recommendation. You neither seek nor want approval or permission from anyone. You are not a people pleaser. You do what you want because it is right for you. You will not be motivated by guilt, threats or peer pressure. You are your own person and nobody tells you what to do. This is not rudeness or arrogance, although it may be perceived that way sometimes. It is simply your world view and you wouldn't have it any other way.

The Self/Other Pattern: Who's it All About Anyway?

If your preference is external, it follows that your attention is on *others*; if your preference is internal, your attention is on *yourself*.

People with *self* preference can behave in ways that take a bit of getting used to. If you have a strong preference for self, other people may find it difficult to talk to you and they may be tempted to reach out and check your pulse for signs of life! You don't express emotion; and people could be forgiven for wondering if you have any deep emotions at all. This is because, during an interaction with another person, you pay attention to *your feelings* and *their facts*. You are not always good with rapport: it doesn't really compute. You don't understand when people get teary-eyed or start sobbing – a lot of the time you wish they'd just get to the point of their story. Heartfelt sympathy, love, care and compassion are all well and good but they're just not your realm. It's not that you're made of stone or anything – it's simply that you check your own internal world so intensely during an interaction, that the other person's feelings often don't come into it. It can be difficult to read you; and your gestures are closed. If people want to know how you're feeling, they have to ask you straight out – otherwise they might never know.

People with a very strong *other* preference are focused on others and are usually full of life! If you have a strong preference for other, you are animated and in tune with the feelings of any other person you interact with. You are clued in to subtle shifts in emotion and you gauge how best to respond to them. An experience in your company leaves the other person feeling understood, appreciated, valued, respected and all the better for having met you. That is, of course, if you operate from the right *intentions* ... And it'd be very unwise not to operate from the right intentions. Rumour has it that your eyes fall out and you lose the power of speech until you change your intentions and start behaving the right way. So I hear, anyway ...

The Sameness/Difference Pattern: Will This Change Anything?

If you have a preference for *sameness*, you are a lot happier when people just leave things as they are and don't go around messing things up! You enjoy routine and you can tolerate change as long as it's gradual. You like the idea of a newer, better, more improved version of yourself, achieved over time. You like consensus and co-operation. You are what is known as a *matcher*.

If you have a preference for *difference*, you like to mix things up! You like to try new things, go to new places and meet different people. Change doesn't bother you at all – sometimes you'll take it on just for the sake of it. You often do a complete overhaul on yourself: new hair sytle, new clothes, new food, anything goes. You love creativity, innovation and diversity. Improvements don't interest you: you'd much prefer to rip it up and start over again. You get bored of people and things very easily. You need to be kept interested and to try new things all the time; otherwise you get impatient and bored.

People with a preference for difference can be either mismatchers or polarity responders. If you are a *mismatcher*, you always notice the exception to the rule and you can always come up with a good counter-argument. You are a good trouble-shooter, too.

If you are a *polarity responder*, you cannot help but do the opposite of what you're told to do. A good friend of mine recently told me that she was suffering from insomnia. She had tried hypnosis and other relaxation techniques to no avail. She has a very active mind and she couldn't seem to sit still long enough to get the benefits of these practices. I gave her a Mind Spa, which is a sound and light machine designed to adjust brainwave frequencies to certain patterns suitable for relaxation, learning, study, concentration and sleep improvement. The machine needs to be put on the appropriate setting for your purpose; different tracks can be chosen. So, relaxation and sleep improvement were the obvious choices for curing my friend's insomnia. I got a call from her a few days after I gave her the machine. She wanted to know if it was alright to listen to the concentration track more than once a day! Focused concentration requires an alert state, which was the exact opposite of my recommendation. My friend is clearly a polarity responder! All I could do was laugh at myself for not having noticed this before. I told her about it and she laughed, too; but whether she decided to listen to the correct tracks or not ... who knows?

The Big Picture/Finer Detail Pattern: Tell Me About It

As you read this section of the book, what are you interested in? Do you want the general gist of what I am saying? Or do you want to know exactly how this section works, and how and where the tools can be applied? Are you interested in the big picture or the finer details?

If you have a preference for the *big picture*, you like summaries, bullet points and overviews. You have a *global preference*. You like it when people get to the point really quickly. You get bored by detail: you are sorting by big picture.

If you have a preference for *finer detail*, for you, the devil is truly in the details. You like information in small chunks; you even reflect this in your language. You use words and phrases like 'precisely', 'exactly', 'specifically', 'piece by piece', 'bit by bit', 'portion', 'size' – anything that adds to the detail. If you are asked a story and someone interrupts you with a question, you go right back to the beginning and start all over again. You love sequence and order. You are happy to explain things step-by-step, in minute detail, because it is important that you leave nothing to chance. You need to get across all the detail. You love to gather information. You think it's good to be kept well-informed so that you know exactly what to do when a situation arises. Your language can seem unemotional at times. This is because your focus is on detail and information. You use lots of qualifiers: the movie wasn't 'good', it was 'very good'; it wasn't 'rubbish', it was 'largely over-rated'. You drive *big picture* people crazy because you take ages to get to the point. They in turn drive *you* crazy: they only tell half the story and they leave out all the important bits!

Exercise: Creative Problem-Solving

Shifting from the finer details up to the big picture, then back down again, is a skill often used to solve problems or plan goals. It is called *chunking up* and *chunking down*. It is a really useful technique for adding perspective.

Think of a goal or problem in your life right now. First, write it out in as much detail as possible. Then do a summary in bullet points, making it as succinct as possible.

This will help you to create an action plan so that you can go for it!

Chunk Down

_____

_____

_____

_____

_____

_____

_____

_____

_____

_____

Chunk Up
- _____
- _____
- _____
- _____

Action Plan

_____

_____

_____

_____

_____

_____

_____

_____

_____

_____

The Convincer Pattern: How Can I Be Sure?

Research suggests that, in general, men are more interested in what a thing *does* than how it looks; women are more interested in how a thing *looks* than what it does. The advertising and marketing worlds are full of examples of this. You need only look at women's high-heeled shoes to know that it's more about how the thing looks than how it functions. Equally, you need only see a man with his faded t-shirt, brown Bermuda shorts, hairy legs, black socks and dirty white running shoes to know that he is on a different level. 'What? It's sunny! I'm too warm. Sure I look fine – who's going to pay any heed, anyway?'

Think of a valuable or important purchase you made recently. Ask yourself what it was that convinced you to buy it. Was it common sense or how the thing made you feel? Some people are convinced by logic and some by emotion. If you are a person who is convinced by *logic*, you examine the facts, features, warranty and functionality. You weigh up the pros and cons before making a commitment. You don't make impulse buys. You want to try things out a number of times to be sure they can perform the intended task. You won't commit until you're sure of this.

If you are a person who is convinced by *emotion*, you check out how something looks, sounds or feels; and then you make a decision. You are governed by your sensory preferences here (see Chapter 3). So, if you have a sight preference, you may view the object; if you have a sound preference, you may listen to a friend's recommendation; if you have a feeling preference, you will want a demonstration.

The Procedures/Options Pattern: How Can I Do It?

Do you prefer order or spontaneity? If you think that there is a right way and a wrong way to do things, you have a preference for *procedure*. You prefer to follow the rules, provided they make sense to you. You are happier doing a job when you know what to do, when to do it, how it should be done and who should be involved. You like to find out how things work so that you can do them correctly. You operate a lot from 'should'. You complain about people not doing as they are told and you get upset when people break the rules. 'Why should they be let away with it when we all have to follow the rules?'

If you have a preference for *options*, you don't mind how the job is done, once it gets done. You are happy with chaos and disorder because it gives you the freedom to make up your own rules. You value your personal freedom and you see rules and regulations as an imposition on that. Ironically, you are often the very one who creates the rules for other people to follow.

Changing Your Preferences and Patterns

Now that you have read through this chapter, you will have an idea of the preferences you most frequently engage. Remember, though: these preferences are governed by *context*. Also, since they are just preferences, they can be changed. Changing your preferences first requires that you become aware of them. From here, you begin to incorporate new preferences into your thinking. As a rule of thumb, when you approach a problem or goal you should always remind yourself that you may only be half-looking at it. The world that you are not familiar with may be the world where you find the difference that makes the difference.

Exercise: Exploring Your Preferences and Patterns

Below are two charts: one for your personal life and one for your professional life. Answer the questions. Examine your completed charts. Compare the two charts. Notice where the opportunities are and begin to work on widening your perspective.

Your Personal Life	Current	Opportunity
What is your sensory preference? See, hear, feel, smell or taste?		
Which do you prefer? People, places, things, activities or information?		
What drives you – pain or pleasure? Moving towards or moving away?		
Is your focus on the opportunity or the threat? Are you proactive or reactive?		
Why do you bother? What's in it for you? Power, connection or achievement?		
In what time frame do you operate? Past, present or future? Short-term, medium-term or long-term?		
How do you sort for feedback? – internally or externally?		
Where is your attention? Self or others?		
Do you like sameness or difference?		
Do you prefer the big picture or finer details?		
How are you convinced? Logic or emotion? Quickly or over time? By look, feel or sound?		
Do you prefer procedures or options?		

Your Professional Life	Current	Opportunity
What is your sensory preference? See, hear, feel, smell or taste?		
Which do you prefer? People, places, things or information?		
What drives you – pain or pleasure? Moving towards or moving away?		
Is your focus on the opportunity or the threat? Are you proactive or reactive?		
Why do you bother? What's in it for you? Power, connection or achievement?		
In what time frame do you operate? Past, present or future? Short-term, medium-term or long-term?		
How do you sort for feedback? – internally or externally?		
Where is your attention? Self or others?		
Do you like sameness or difference?		
Do you prefer the big picture or finer details?		
How are you convinced? Logic or emotion? Quickly or over time? By look, feel or sound?		
Do you prefer procedures or options?		

CHAPTER 7

Keeping Extraordinary Relationships

How far you go in life depends on you being tender with the young, compassionate with the aged, sympathetic with the striving, and tolerant of the weak and the strong. Because someday in life you will have been all of these.

George Washington Carver

The Quality of Your Relationships

If there is one thing I would single out as being the most important for quality of life (after the basic needs are met), it is the quality of your personal relationships. In previous chapters, we explored the personal needs, wants and desires. We learned skills that can add to your understanding of people, particularly in the context of interaction. We examined all of the ways in which we can engage more effectively and create the foundations for extraordinary relationships. It's worth remembering, though, that *creating* extraordinary relationships is actually the easier part. Most of us are open and interested in people that are open and interested in us. Therefore the real challenge comes in *keeping* the relationship after the initial groundwork has been done.

People often treat the second stage of a relationship like the second bite of a bar of chocolate. Somehow, it becomes less appetising the more of it there is. The internal dialogue can go something like this: 'I've done enough now. I went to all that bother of getting the ball rolling, so it's up to him/her from here on in.' In reading this chapter, I want you to explore the process that takes place not just at the beginning of a relationship but as time goes on. My hope for you is that you master the art of maintaining extraordinary relationships and that your life improves because of this.

Relationship Needs

Relationships are driven by our need for *connection*, *impact* and *affection*. We all want to feel that we belong and we all want to feel that we have control over our world. We also want to know that we can influence others without losing their love or affection. When we make judgments about the quality of our relationships, we are usually referring to the presence or absence of one or all of these three needs. These needs are sought to varying degrees in all of our relationships, including those with our partners, family members, friends, bosses, colleagues and acquaintances.

Sometimes our need to be in a relationship is so strong that we will stay in it no matter how bad it gets. Unfortunately, many of us are guilty of giving up on our relationships and pulling back from them but not leaving them physically. This is because relationships rarely come as a stand-alone package. There are always additional benefits. A relationship can provide us with a sense of identity, give us a role to play, allow us certain freedoms and provide us with safety. It is not so surprising then that certain people hang on in there, way past the relationship's sell-by date. Relationships are interdependent, dynamic and organic things. They are constantly evolving or devolving; and they always require attention. It is normal for relationships to gradually build or decline and, unless there is a huge breach of values, it is unusual for relationships to come to an abrupt and sudden end.

Time

Time plays an important part in our relationships. Some relationships go back a long way but they are no longer given any time. Some relationships go back a long way and they are actively avoided, but because there is a history there, the chord will not be severed fully regardless of what discomfort is felt on meeting each other. It's fair enough to say that you can measure the importance of a relationship by the amount of time you choose to give it.

Intimacy

Intimacy can be divided into three categories: *intellectual*, *emotional* and *physical*. It is possible for a person to be intimate in all three ways with another person. In choosing a life partner, it's important to have intimacy of every kind. Intimacy varies in different relationships. A relationship can be intimate in one category and not in the next. Different relationships will be intimate to differing degrees. So, you could share a degree of intellectual intimacy with a teacher but you wouldn't dream of going in for a hug. You could share an emotional intimacy with a close friend of the same sex. You could have a friend who shares your deepest, darkest secrets but you may not rank them intellectually.

Most of us are part of different social circles and each circle provides different forms of connection. Intimacy can be extended to the people you meet every day but, obviously, the depth and breadth of the intimacy will differ with each interaction. If you meet your local shopkeeper, you may share a level of intimacy in talking about your personal wellbeing but she may still remain on the level of acquaintance in your mind. So, we don't need to have deep intimacy in every relationship in order for us to interact. If our intimacy needs are satisfied in a few different relationships, we usually avoid seeking new ones.

Affinity

The functionality of our relationships is shaped by whether or not we actually like the other person. Not all relationships require mutual liking but, in order for them to exist, they do require a level of understanding and mutual agreement. Think about a strained employer–employee relationship: it can exist with neither party liking the other but both parties being prepared to work together because of the recognition that there are mutual benefits. Unfortunately, this can also happen with life partners: a relationship breaks down and all that remains are the mutual benefits. This is where the 'stick it out for the kids' mentality comes in. Obviously, this is not healthy. There are crossovers within the family; and the emotional state of each parent affects everybody involved.

Control

Control is on the top of the agenda for most people. When people comment on other relationships, they speak about who is 'wearing the trousers' and who is 'under the thumb'. Evidence shows that influence and power in any relationship are not always equal to both parties. There is an interplay that occurs and this determines a relationship's functionality. Researchers have defined relationship control in three categories: complementary, symmetrical and parallel.

Complementary relationships are based on difference. When two people come together they complement each other's needs for expression and effectively become a single unit. One cannot survive without the other. In this relationship, each participant knows their role. Each person has their function and each person must subscribe fully if the relationship is to work. A traditional form of complementary relationships is when a man works outside the home and a woman is a stay-at-home mother. These relationships are not always equal, though. The big challenge with them is that individual needs are sacrificed at the expense of the group need.

This is not the case in *symmetrical* relationships. These relationships are based on equality. Each partner contributes equally to the relationship and each partner benefits equally as a result. In this type of relationship, each partner holds separate identities in and outside of the relationship. So, they come together for certain things and they separate for others. They may even have separate interests: 'I let him do his thing and he lets me do mine.'

The *parallel* relationship mixes elements of complementary and symmetrical relationships. It is the best of the three structures because it allows for more flexibility and accommodation of each partner's needs. Partners are committed to each another and share common goals, but they also pursue personal interests. Each partner complements the other and makes up for the shortcomings of the other when required. This type of relationship calls for a higher degree of mutual commitment and respect. Here, one plus one makes *three*. The relationship becomes more than the sum of its parts. There are no white knights and no doormats here. Neither party is 'under the thumb'. There is respect, commitment and sharing.

In order for relationships to be healthy, there must be a common bond. There must be knowledge that the other partner has your interests at heart; they 'have your back', so to speak. This is the substance of great, long-lasting relationships. In an extraordinary relationship, nobody 'falls in love': both partners find love in each other. They want to be together, not because of what they get from the relationship, but because of how it *feels* to be in the relationship. Each partner has a respect for the organic nature of a relationship and they actively work to protect and enrich it. Flexibility, commitment, active compassion, mutual understanding and respect are the hallmarks of extraordinary relationships.

The Emotional Tone of Your Relationships

In Chapter 5, we looked at the non-verbal factors that influence communication, i.e. body language. It doesn't take a rocket scientist to figure out that what we say and *how* we say it can dramatically change the meaning of our message and how it is received.

Let's say your partner asks, 'Are you alone?' This could mean very different things depending on the tone of the question and the way in which it is asked:

- It could mean your partner fears that you are in potential danger.
- It could mean your partner wants to hold a private conversation with you.
- If could be an invitation to ... you know ...?

Our tone of voice and our body language will communicate our feelings. Tone of voice alone can convey annoyance, anger, friendliness, playfulness, distance, arrogance – a whole range of emotions.

What is being said and *how* it is being said impact on a relationship experience. Psychologists refer to this as *meta communication*. Meta programs and body language are elements of this meta communication. A meta communication is a communication that affects another communication system.

What Attracts Us Into a Relationship?

You know what they say: you can't choose your family but you can choose your friends. There are many factors that govern our decision to form a relationship with another person. The most obvious factors are shared interests and likeability. Below, we will examine seven reasons that might attract us into having a relationship with another person.

How You Look

You will hear many a person proclaim that they do not judge a book by its cover; in reality, that is not altogether true. Our initial attraction to people is on the basis of how they look. Research shows that people who are considered to be physically attractive do better in life than those who are not. Apparently, this is hardwired into us. Beautiful men and women tend to be viewed as more successful, pleasant, interesting, strong, modest and exciting. However, before you decide that you are bunched, research also shows that people who have reasonable looks (whatever that means) and a good personality fair better in the long-term. While attractiveness is important for drawing attention, keeping this attention requires you to have aspects of your personality in order. It makes sense when you think of it. How many times have you been underwhelmed on seeing a movie star interviewed? They can be stunning on screen and a complete let-down in real life. Sometimes a screenwriter's imagination comes up with something far more attractive than the reality.

We cannot ignore the importance of appearance, though: that's why personal grooming and hygiene are so important if you are looking for a relationship. I have a friend who is convinced that men decide whether or not they like a woman by her looks. This is only true to a certain extent and in context, but men certainly are visual creatures. Knowing this might mean you are less offended when you are in a man's company and he scans the room to have a good look at everyone. He can't help it: it's just in his nature.

How You Compare

We like people who like us; and we like people who are like us. We enjoy the similarity. Research shows that age, education, race, religion, economic background and status are similar in most couples. I have found that most relationship issues I encounter in my practice can be traced back to cultural differences. These differences are originally viewed as idiosyncrasies and are overlooked in the initial stages of the relationship, especially if the people have a preference for sorting by difference. However, these issues rise to the fore later on when *value clashes* occur. There is interesting research on this and it shows that, in general, personality discrepancies will be tolerated above value discrepancies.

In relationships, there are many reasons why we are drawn to what we have in common. It gives us a sense of certainty if we can understand and predict with relative accuracy the needs, wants and desires of our partner. This reduces tension. Also, when we connect with this person it validates and affirms who *we* are. The fact that we are accepted, understood and liked makes us feel confident and safe in our identity.

How You 'Complete' Me

After reading about the strength of relationships between people who have a lot in common, you'd be forgiven for thinking that the 'opposites attract' theory now doesn't hold much weight; but this is not the case. On entering relationships, many of us are not our evolved selves. Some of us bring a lot of baggage with us. Relationships function if there is overall balance and consent – good old 'division of labour'. There must be agreement and understanding in the distribution of roles. Of course, people sometimes sign up to dysfunctional relationships and consent to damaging roles: the man earns the money and the woman is told how to spend it; the man is the boss and the woman is the slave; the woman is the princess and the man is the servant; the woman makes the decisions and informs the man afterwards. You will see evidence of these relationships everywhere, even to the extreme of the 'battered wife': the man must be served and the woman must obey. These are all complementary roles; each partner functions to serve the other's needs, nuances or shortcomings. You can't have a princess without a servant; and you can't have a boss without a slave.

What You Do For Me

You have seen it and squirmed and commented on it: the aging billionaire with the young, leggy blonde for a wife. No matter how often they proclaim their love for each other, you think differently … Many people enter into a relationship on the grounds of *exchange*. They are prepared to give of themselves in order to get what they want. This happens in business all the time: 'I'll put up with your silly requests because, in the end, I get what I want, too.' This is transactional and can be unemotional – but it is done outside the realm of business, too. It can be done with emotion and it can be one of the factors holding a relationship together.

What You Can Do

Confidence, competence, humour and cash: now *that's* a combination many a person will be happy to find! We like to be around competent people. We like to learn from them and be impressed by them. However, we are attracted to a mix of competence and imperfection, too. We like people to be really good at many things but we need them to be imperfect, too. We need to bring them down to our level. Their quirks and idiosyncrasies help us to do that. So, the nutty professor who trips up on his way to the podium is more endearing to us. Think about how many movies you've seen where the super-cool, perfect guy makes a big blunder but eventually redeems himself to get the girl. The moviemakers do their research: it's the old 'beautiful but flawed' thing and it is very attractive. So, if you're trying to impress a woman with your intelligence, make sure you spill your tea on yourself while you're at it – *after* you've stunned her with your luminous brilliance, of course. And if you're a glorious goddess of heavenly beauty, make sure you look utterly divine as you trip over your handbag on the way to the loo.

What You Share With Me

The late Gerry Ryan once mentioned that, when he was young, he gauged his friendships on whether or not he was 'on farting terms' with the other person! I suppose that would reveal something about a relationship, alright. Relationships are built on trust and respect; and our *disclosure* is an indication of the level of trust and respect. The more you are prepared to tell me about yourself, the more I feel validated, important and maybe even special. Everyone loves a secret; and they really love being the only one who knows a secret about someone else because that puts them in a higher rank. Naturally, the type of secret will be important, too. A deep secret that makes a person vulnerable carries far more weight than a minor disclosure.

There is a time and place for sharing secrets – and you must be especially wise to this in the early stages of a relationship. There is also an appropriate amount to reveal; and it needs to be reciprocal. The amount that one person shares must be in line with the amount that the other person shares. Let's say I tell you that I am nervous for the first five minutes of any seminar. You then tell me you are nervous when you have to give a presentation at work. Then you decide that you like me and you start to pour out every secret and every insecurity you have ever had. That really is 'coming on too strong' and it's usually a major turn-off. Remember: it is flawed beauty, *not damaged goods*, that will attract people. Nobody likes neediness. If you see that level of neediness in yourself, you need to knock it on the head or do some work with a therapist. Kick it to the kerb for once and for all!

Where You Are

Boring and all as it may sound, most relationships are formed with people that we simply encounter frequently: people we work with, people we live near or people we meet on a regular basis. You have heard that 'familiarity breeds contempt'. It does – but it can also breed attraction. We are more likely to create friendships and build relationships with those people we encounter often.

The Six Stages of Relationship Growth

Mark L. Knapp was a renowned professor who researched and wrote extensively on the subject of communication in relationships. In his book *Interpersonal Communication and Human Relationships*, he identified the stages of relationship growth. The following section is loosely based on Knapp's findings.

Stage One: Breaking the Ice

You see someone you are interested in and you would like to communicate, but you need a signal to show this. This is where simple eye contact, a smile or a handshake comes in. You may decide to walk right up to the person and say hello. Many people fear this, though. They worry about running out of things to say. They worry that the other person could leave them stranded and walk away, if the advances are unwanted. In my practice, I teach people to have an exit strategy as well as an entry strategy. A good approach is to show an interest, try to chat but also have a place you can go to if things don't go to plan. This can be as simple as being prepared to say: 'Goodbye; it was nice meeting you.'

Stage Two: Exploring

Placing too much or too little emphasis on stage two is not practical. This is the *screening* or *discounting* phase. This is where each party decides if they want to get to know the other person better. There is a *meta communication* part to this transaction. It is barely about what you are saying; it is mainly about what you are interpreting from the situation. This is why 'small talk' is necessary. Many of my clients are single and I have to convince them of the value of small talk when trying to find a partner. You just can't get deep into talk with most people without walking through the 'small talk' phase first. That is the other person's safety net; and your job is to get permission to pass through it. The way you do that is by letting them engage in 'small talk' with you for a while. You can talk about the weather or any other subject that is inoffensive and non-threatening. Your job is to make the person feel safe, happy and well liked. Absolutely no criticism, unless it is obviously playful and easy to interpret. Avoid dismissals or negativity as well – they can be very off-putting.

Stage Three: Intensifying

It might take you some time to get past stage two. It could take a few meetings and a fair bit of small talk but, after that, you may be given permission to move to stage three: intensifying. It is in this stage that your knowledge of body language and meta programs will come in handy. This is the mutual self-disclosure stage. At this stage, you move from acquaintance to familiarity. The formalities are gone and you have developed a mutual understanding around lots of things. If you have really intensified, you will be expressing feelings of connection and appreciation for one another: 'It's so great that we are getting to know each other', 'We are just like peas in a pod', etc.

Stage Four: Integrating

At this point in the relationship, you become an established couple. You go to social events together, you share property together, you may move in together. You move into a phase where 'what's mine is yours and what's yours is mine' – once the relationship is healthy, of course. This is the stage where you assume a common identity and your individual interests merge, as do your characters. You complement each other and you look out for each other.

Stage Five: Bonding

If this was a business relationship, you would formalise it and set things on a legal footing at an early stage. In a personal relationship, this kind of formality comes later. It is the time when you get engaged or married – or you decide to formalise your relationship in another way.

Stage Six: Differentiating

In this stage, the bonding has occurred, the common ground has been integrated and the relationship is well established. It is at this time that there may be a search to recover your individuality, while keeping the relationship going in a healthy way. In a strong relationship, this is a good thing; in an unstable relationship, this can lead to major problems or even dissolution. This is the time when finger-pointing and blame can come in. Feelings of tension and discomfort surface while one partner (or perhaps both) attempts to reassert their individuality. Many relationships survive this challenge and go on to reach a form of semi-stationary plateau. Here, the relationship remains in a relatively stable social system for the duration of the partners' lives.

The Four Stages of Relationship Decline

Sometimes relationships do not thrive or even survive. When this is the case, the relationship goes into decline. There are four stages of relationship decline.

Stage One: Circumscribing

This is the beginning of the end. If the partners fail to address each other's needs in the relationship, the relationship stops growing and the cracks begin to appear. As tensions remain unresolved or unexpressed, one or both partners go into a form of *denial*. Everything carries on as normal on the surface but the romantic side declines and the time-sharing element reduces dramatically. Daydreaming and fantasy become more frequent. The partners may withdraw from the relationship and stop giving it energy. Conversations are reduced and input is diminished. Silences grow as both partners retreat into themselves but carry on regardless.

Stage Two: Stagnation

If stage one is allowed to continue, the energy is completely drained from the relationship and it loses its dynamic altogether. The relationship effectively becomes a shadow play: all of the movements and all of the engagements, but none of the affection, compassion and energy required to keep it alive as an organic entity.

Stage Three: Avoidance

Stagnation turns to irritation; irritation turns to dissatisfaction; dissatisfaction turns to discomfort; and so, the solution is *distance*. The partners may deliberately engage in behaviour designed to avoid. They may avoid contact or proximity. They may even avoid being in the same place at the same time. At this point, the relationship has run its course and it's all over, bar the shouting. It's time for someone to pack their bags and leave.

Stage Four: Finishing Up

When a relationship declines to stage four, the wrap-up may be cordial, technical and even relatively unemotional. However, many relationships do not take that exact course. Sometimes one partner wants out but the other doesn't. In this case, there will be conflict. The rejected partner may get angry, upset and annoyed. They may even seek vengeance for the other partner's perceived betrayal. If one partner wreaks vengeance, this just affirms for the other partner that the decision to terminate the relationship was correct. The partner who has chosen to terminate the relationship may demonise the other partner, using this to deflect from any feelings of guilt. It can take a lot of time to get past this stage and dissolve the relationship.

Relationship Systems

Not all relationships are romantic ones and not all interpersonal dynamics are the same. What follows is an outline of five of the most common relationship systems. Relationship systems affect emotional expression: the members in a particular system depend on the presence of a certain structure to achieve maximum output and effectiveness.

Conjunct Relationships

Conjunct relationships are relationships where the partners agree on everything. This is not healthy. A good relationship has differences and has ways of dealing with those differences. I know of a mother–son relationship where the mother agrees with *everything* that the son says or does. He can do no wrong in her eyes. Completely unaware, this mother is actually causing her son untold frustration: he feels he cannot have a conversation with her without it being affirmed. There is therefore no debate, no conflict, no discussion of ideas – just total agreement. At first glance, most people would see that there is something a bit 'off' with that. Try it for yourself: ask your partner to have a conversation with you where they agree with absolutely everything you say. Your experience of the conversation will be very revealing: you'll see that it really lacks sincerity and energy.

Opposite Relationships

Opposite relationships exist when one partner constantly contradicts the other partner. This is obviously a *mismatcher* (see Chapter 6). It plays out like this: when he talks about a great idea he has, she sees only the problems with it; when she is upset, he is happy; when he wants to go out, she decides she wants to stay home, etc. This type of relationship is easily predicted so, with a little effort, it can be managed. All it involves is a little forethought and some reverse psychology.

You may ask *why* anyone would be involved in a relationship like this, since it seems so draining. Sometimes the relationship can be so strong in other areas (common direction and values) that this aspect can be overlooked.

Triangular Relationships

Most of us have been involved in a triangular relationship at some stage. As the name suggests, this relationship depends on the presence of three people for its dynamic. When all three are present, discussion and banter are in full swing. The actors bring out the best in one another and the interaction generates debate, laughter and entertainment. However, let's say that on a night out one of the three members leaves early: the conversation takes a nose dive! The two remaining people feel awkward and disconnected without the third person's presence.

Square Relationships

This type of relationship requires four members for it to operate at full capacity. Let's say that on a night out, two of the four people arrive first. They begin to argue and bicker. Then the third member shows up but they just observe the bickering. The two arguing members become the focus of the third member but it is at their expense. It is not until the fourth member arrives that there is real productivity and creative output.

Dyad Relationships

A dyad relationship is where a couple is effectively viewed as being the one entity: Jim and Mary, Ben and Bob, Karen and Sue, etc. A dyad offers security, since there is strength in numbers. Research shows that women are happier to be consumed by a dyad until they reach their forties; whereas men want to assert their individuality until they reach their forties. After that, both parties switch preferences: men want to be consumed by the dyad and women want to reassert their independence.

Keeping Your Relationship Special

Even if you are lucky enough to have a romantic relationship that is healthy and fulfilling, you should still do some work on it. The tips below are sure to help your relationship thrive!

- Actively work towards making your partner happy.
- Invest time in the relationship. Create time exclusively for your partner as often as you can – at least twice a week.
- Commit to the relationship. Be a couple and integrate fully, while remaining true to yourself.
- Remember who you are; and be who you are.
- Do lots of things together, from the mundane to the very special.
- Understand what your partner values; and work to meet those values.
- Be prepared to stand up for your partner when they are not able to do it themselves.
- Keep your partner informed of all your news, achievements and successes as they happen.
- Show your partner that you support them emotionally.
- Demonstrate your trust in your partner. You can do this by confiding in them.
- Be prepared to offer and give help when your partner needs it.
- Make your partner feel liked, loved, special, important, valued, needed and wanted.
- Be caring, honest and loyal. You must be capable of holding their confidence.
- Demonstrate empathy and understanding.
- Listen to your partner and hear what they are saying.
- Talk to your partner every day.
- Tell your partner how you feel about them.
- Find out how your partner wants to be loved and cared for.
- Teach your partner how to love and care for you.
- Work together through good and bad times.
- Ask for help when you need it and accept help when it's offered.
- Surprise your partner! Amuse them, have fun with them and flirt with them often.
- Discuss the state of your relationship.
- Avoid taking anything for granted. Work to improve something in your relationship every day.
- Include your partner. Involve them and allow them to influence, affect and love you.
- Help your partner to achieve their desires, goals and dreams.

Exercise: Relationship Audit

Do an audit on your relationship with your life partner. If you are not in a romantic relationship, do the audit with a friendship that really matters to you.

Remember that your partner must first give you *permission* if you are to help them with their interests, needs, wants and possibilities.

Interests	What are your partner's interests?	How can you help them meet those interests?
Likes		
Loves		
Passions		
Inspirations		
Joys		
Hobbies		
Projects		

Needs	What are your partner's needs?	How can you help them meet those needs?
Safety		
Connection		
Code		
Identity		
Competence		
Impact		
Freedom		

Wants	What are your partner's wants?	How can you help them meet those wants?
Empathy		
Pleasure		

Creative Expression		
Goals		

Possibilities	What are your partner's possibilities?	How can you help them meet those possibilities?
Growth		
Contribution		
Peak performance		
Transcendence		

CHAPTER 8

Getting Past What's Stopping You

> *It's not who you are that holds you back,*
> *it's who you think you're not.*
> **Anonymous**

Have you ever been awakened by the sounds that come with the breaking of dawn? You hear the birds beginning to sing and flutter their tiny little wings. You watch the beautiful morning light flow into your bedroom, reminding you that another day is about to begin. Do you suddenly sit upright, kick back the sheets and leap out onto the floor, a big bright smile on your face? There you are in your cotton PJs, stretching your arms high above your head and saying, 'Hello, world! I'm back! Did you miss me? Oh, we are going to have such a fantastic day together. And aren't you so lucky to have me? Don't I just make you sparkle?' Off you skip downstairs to eat your Pop-Tarts and take a mouthful of tea before you take on the day ... If your average morning is like this, you need *help*. And please don't ring me; I'm not available.

Maybe your mornings are more like those of Jack Black's character in *School of Rock*. Do you raise your stunned, grumpy head from under the sheets, scan the room through bleary eyes, mumble incoherently and then pull the sheets over you again, hoping that you won't have to get up until the crack of noon? If that's the case, you could probably do with feeling a bit more extraordinary; and hopefully this chapter will help you to get the wind back in your sail.

You don't want to be going around so full of gusto that you approach every single moment with a tornado of enthusiasm. (If that *is* what you want, there are pills that can do that, you know?) But do you know that feeling when an exciting event lifts your spirit and your energy? Have you experienced those times when you want to get going, when you want to get on with it? These are the times when your goals light your fire! In this chapter, we'll reflect on those times in your life and we'll explore what opportunities are here for you now to create a life that is that exciting. You'll see that your life can be so much more interesting, enthusiastic, energetic, creative and positive. You won't end up leaping about, ranting and raving in a feel-good frenzy; that would just be annoying. But you could end up creating a gentle stream of enthusiasm that serves as a backdrop to your life. Wouldn't it be nice to look to the horizon and be filled with genuine interest; to have a zest and curiosity about you; and a hope that things can get better? I want you to be able to stand on the edge of your universe and be filled with wonder. I want you to have both feet firmly planted in reality while your thoughts are infused with possibility.

Here's the thing: most people do not live extraordinary lives because they do not believe that they are extraordinary people. Much of our conditioning makes us question our own abilities:

- 'Who do you think you are?'
- 'You're just like the rest of us.'
- 'You think you're something special?'
- 'What are you like?'

Let's focus on that last question: 'What are you like?' Let me tell you what you are like. You *are* like the rest of us – but if you think there's nothing special about you, that's just a poor decision. You can be as special as you want to be, provided you begin *treating yourself* that way. You could wait around for a hero to come along and do things for you but he might take a while … In the meantime, why not get on with it yourself? And think about this: if you are 'like the rest of us', that puts you in some really great company. You are like Einstein. You are like Mozart. You are like the Dalai Lama. You are like Oprah. You are the same as all of these people, just because you are a person.

You are the same; but different in some ways, maybe. Maybe you are different in that you have never considered what you are capable of. Maybe you are different in that you haven't realised that you have as much a right as any of these people to do what you want to do with your life; to be who you want to be. Yes, you may feel trapped. Yes, you may think that it is stupid to expect so much more from yourself. Yes, you might feel like it's too late. But here is the *truth*: it is never too late to be the best you can be. It is never too late to breathe life into your dreams and most of all it is never too late to start believing in yourself.

A major obstacle that people face in trying to lead an extraordinary life is that, while we love the idea of success, we also fear it. We ask, 'What happens if I don't make it? Will I look stupid? What will happen even if I do succeed? Will I still fit in? Will I still have friends? Will I always have to be better?' There are many reasons why people fear success. All of them are backed by fear and designed to keep you from claiming the best out of life. We put up barriers to our own success. These barriers are held in place because we arrived at a conclusion and we stopped developing our thinking around it any further. We sometimes see our situation as a *fait accompli* instead of realising that life is a process. Success is a process. Thinking is a process; and beliefs are frozen processes but are actually open to movement. You need to learn how to shift your thinking beyond what you have *decided* is the truth. This chapter will show you how.

To get you where you deserve to be you will need to question some deeply held assumptions. I can't know what your assumptions are but I can give you the tools to figure it out for yourself. The fact that you will learn these tools for yourself will mean that you can pass them on to someone else and bring some inspiration to their lives, too.

So, let me ask you the following questions:
- Could you be an extraordinary person?
- Could you be an exceptional human being?
- Could you change the world?
- Could you be as successful as Bono?
- Could you be as wealthy as Bill Gates?
- Could you be as influential as Oprah Winfrey?
- Could you be as compassionate as Mother Teresa?
- Could you be as skilful as Johnny Depp?
- Could you do what these people have already done? Could you live an extraordinary life?

In thinking about what you *could* be, also ask yourself what you *want*.
- Do you want to be the best that you can be?
- Do you want to be the best mum, dad or friend?
- Do you want to be the best musician in the world?
- Do you want to be the best coach in the world?
- Do you want to be the best at whatever it is you already do in the world?

What you may not have realised is that each of these things involves the same thing! Each question points towards a *limitation*. The limitation is your belief about it. Once you decide you can or you can't, you have already closed the lid on your potential to a point. What I want to do here is to give you the tools to *remove limitation* so that, whatever your choice is you are free to make it. Whether you choose to use this book as a way of improving your job, home life or your relationships is up to you. You create the definition of what extraordinary is in your life; and we will take the rest from there.

For a moment, assume that there are no obstacles – real or imagined – in your life. What would you do if you could only succeed? How would you make your life an exceptional one? How would you make the leap from ordinary to extraordinary? What would you focus on? How would you know when you got there? Let's set aside any major critical analysis for now: just let your beliefs take a back seat for a moment. Instead, enter your thoughts into the Dream Machine and allow your subconscious to get to work immediately.

Exercise: The Dream Machine

To make my life extraordinary, I would...	What would have to be done in order for that to happen?	How would I know when I have it?

What is a Belief?

In doing the Dream Machine exercise, you have already begun to measure your options against your beliefs. If you believe that your options are possible, you will go ahead and chase them. If you think not, you will park them into the realm of fantasy and hope somehow that your subconscious will mysteriously bring them about for you.

Beliefs that hold you back are self-imposed limitations. Even if you have been directly or inadvertently handed down the belief, the fact that you have accepted it causes it to be *self-imposed*.

Beliefs are different from facts. Facts are indisputable. Beliefs are not. Facts operate from logic and universal principles. Beliefs are subjective and are often coloured by your feelings. For instance: I say that I am a man; that is a fact. I say that I am a great man; that is also a fact. Just kidding! That is simply an *opinion* that I have stated as a fact. That opinion reflects my belief around my idea of myself.

Simply saying that I am great doesn't necessarily mean that I am great. However, it will cause me to *behave* in a way that may actually result in me becoming great. Now, if I say I am great and I don't believe that statement, no matter how often I repeat it, it will make absolutely no difference. Some people say that repeating what you *want* to be true will train your subconscious to make it become habit. That is simply not true. The only habit that will be created is the habit of *saying* it.

The real change will only occur the moment you believe in it, and not a second before. Only then does it *become a fact in your mind*. And to add to that, whether you believe in a fact or not does not change the fact that it is a fact! For example, it makes no difference if I do not believe that the world is round: it will still be round. If you do not believe that you have the power to revolutionise your life, that does not alter the fact that you have the power. You have the ability, you have the resources and you usually don't even have to use as much of your ability as you might think.

The thing about beliefs is that they *feel* as if they are true; and therein lies the problem. Our beliefs are often masked as facts but they are just opinions or assumptions. Beliefs satisfy your overwhelming drive for certainty; and this can produce major limitations. We like to know that we understand what is happening to us. We like to feel that we have a handle on most things. We need to feel that we are in control, at least to a certain degree. But sometimes we believe in things *too much*. I've always liked what Robert Anton Wilson had to say about this: 'Belief is the death of intelligence.'

Strong beliefs produce a narrower focus of attention. Strong belief excludes options. This very limitation can also be the driving force for greatness. Muhammad Ali believed that he was the greatest and now most of us believe that, too. Will Smith believes that once an idea is formed in your mind, it has already happened to you and you just have to wait for the effect to show up in the physical world. His life is a testimony to that belief. Bruce Lee believed that you have to *let go* of the weight of your mind in order to produce flow. His actions were an exquisite demonstration of this freedom of mind. So, while beliefs are simply our interpreted distortions of reality, many of these distortions can be good for us. Belief is the air that fans the flames. Belief is what sets you on fire. Belief is the fuel behind emotional ignition. The effect of beliefs can be far reaching and long lasting, for good and bad. Depending on the nature of your beliefs, they can bring you to greatness or they can hold you back forever.

It makes sense to examine how our beliefs are formed, how they are 'normed' and how they can be changed and replaced with more empowering ones. Every day as you go about your business, things are happening all around you. Some of these things draw your attention; others don't even get a look in. Sometimes, a person calls your name and your attention goes straight to them. Sometimes you don't even hear a person calling your name because you are so interested in other things (think of your mother calling you in for dinner when you were playing a game as a child). All of these things happen to you, whether you are aware of them or totally oblivious to them. If you are 'oblivious', it simply means that you are not paying deliberate or conscious attention to something. But that doesn't stop your subconscious from taking it all in like a sponge, anyway. The fact is, you are constantly being bombarded with information and, in order to handle it, your brain needs to manage it in some way. It does this by *filtering out* large portions of it from your awareness; if it didn't your senses would be overloaded.

The process of filtering incoming information is done through three key processes: Deletion, Distortion and Generalisation. These filters are not completely separate from each other; in fact, they overlap. But they give you a useful way of looking at how you handle all this information. The downside of these filters is that they compact and reduce the incoming information. This causes us to make errors in judgment. It can cause us to come up with poor assumptions and deductions, which in turn lead to dodgy belief systems. Fortunately, the world of NLP offers a counter system that will help you to recover lost data and make better decisions in the light of more useful information.

Before we learn how to get past the filters, let's take a look at them in operation.

Deletion
(is selective)

This is a process of selective attention. Your attention is placed on certain things but excludes others.

Positive example: Successfully meditating while ignoring the noise of traffic outside.

Negative example: Refusing to go to Australia because of your fear of spiders.

Worth keeping in mind: Is there anything you are not paying attention to that might make a difference?

Distortion
(affects accuracy)

This is a process where you change the meaning of what is happening to you to make it fit in with your understanding of the world.

Positive example: Becoming fully absorbed and emotionally affected while watching a movie.

Negative example: Being told things are bad and letting your imagination conjure up all sorts of doomsday scenarios.

Worth keeping in mind: What have you altered and is it useful to you?

**Generalisation
(produces assumptions)**

This is a process whereby you make assumptions or combine things to create meaning about what is happening in your world.

Positive example: Going to a particular therapist and concluding that all therapy works.

Negative example: Experiencing two unhappy romantic relationships and concluding that there is no point in ever having a relationship.

Worth keeping in mind: Does the logic hold in all situations?

Key point

It is important to remember that, as the information is being filtered it is not going onto a clean plate. Everything that you are experiencing is being affected by and is affecting your inner world. What you pay attention to in the first place and the meanings you come up with are triggered by your existing beliefs, values and memories. So much so, that you will often change the meaning of what is happening so that it fits in with your existing beliefs.

Remember that, as you experience your world you are *choosing* what you are paying attention to. First you notice something, then you attach meaning to it, then you combine both of these things to make assumptions and arrive at conclusions. The result is that you end up feeling certain you have understood what is going on. Because you feel you have understood it, you believe in it – good, bad or indifferent. If you make a statement about it, you have already thought it through; and in your mind it is a fact. Really, all you are doing is communicating or explaining that fact. It is not meant to be open for debate and you don't like it when it is, because this messes with your feeling of certainty. This is what I like to call our 'God Complex'.

The God Complex

The God Complex is there to give us that feeling of competence and certainty in the world but also to protect us from losing face and feeling foolish. This is a certainty we humans crave and it often brings with it a certain arrogance. Think about the last time you were in an argument or someone challenged one of your beliefs. You most probably went on the defensive straight away. If you were to look behind your argument you would probably reveal the following positions:

- *I am right about this. I wouldn't have said it if I wasn't!*
- *I am right because I am intelligent; and if you say any different you are wrong because I am not stupid – but you just might be!*
- *I am right and even if I was wrong at the time I wouldn't have been if you had not upset me, distracted me and confused me. So really I was right all along!*
- *If I did get it wrong it was only because I was in a bad place at the time so I wasn't really myself, which means that I was in the right.*
- *Even if I say I am wrong that means I am right about being wrong, which means that I am right.*

This degree of conviction will, predictably, provoke emotion if challenged. This is one of the key reasons that people fail to change their belief, even in the light of new information. Keep this in mind as we return to an examination of the three filters.

How the Filters Work

Here is an example that demonstrates how all three filters can affect and shape a single experience.

Deletion

Deletion is a bit like buying a pair of trainers that are not waterproofed: you only find about it when it's already raining. Deletion is all about *selective attention*. Let's look at deletion in action in regard to a thought:

How can I be extraordinary? I am going through a bit of a rough patch at the minute and everything is all over the place.

If you ask the following questions, you will begin to notice the deletions.

- What is missing from the statement?
- What has been left out?
- What is not being said?

The speaker has not explained what 'extraordinary' means to them. They have not described what the 'rough patch' is. They have not told us what 'everything' is. And they have not explained what they mean by the phrase 'all over the place'. There are other deletions inherent in the statement. The persons says they are going through a rough patch but there are likely to be plenty of areas of their life that are actually going well – they just haven't paid any attention to that.

Distortion

If we have used selective attention, we are working with limited information and we begin the process of labelling things: *this* is A and *that* is B. However, our labelling can be incorrect and our descriptions can be inaccurate. Distortion is all about accuracy – or rather, the lack of it.

Read the same statement again:

How can I be extraordinary? I am going through a bit of a rough patch at the minute and everything is all over the place.

What happens when you visualise the speaker acting out this statement in a *literal* way? What do you see when they say, 'I am going through a rough patch'? Can you actually see a rough patch? Can you touch it, hold it, feel it?

What comes to you when they say 'and everything is all over the place'? Is everything all over the place? Is that in the rough patch or in everything? If it is, then what's wrong with that? What has changed meaning? Is anything being exaggerated?

When you take things literally, you begin to notice the metaphors, descriptions and labels. These are critically important in deciphering meaning – but they are *distortions*. The statement lends itself to being taken further:

> *How could I be extraordinary? Sure, I am just an ordinary run of the mill, bog standard person.*

Something has been distorted and has lost its literal meaning. It has been assigned an incorrect label. The 'rough patch' is a just a metaphor, as is 'run of the mill' and 'bog standard'. The person was not actually standing in a rough patch at the time of the statement. They weren't actually going anywhere in the moment of that statement. No more than they were of 'bog standard', whatever that is supposed to signify.

Generalisation

Because we now have selective attention and altered meanings, we arrive at certain conclusions. We have established a belief that gives us a degree of comfort. This belief will now justify our actions.

Read the same statement a final time:

> *How can I be extraordinary? I am going through a bit of a rough patch at the minute and everything is all over the place.*

Ask yourself this question: how has this person combined their experience to come up their statement? They connected 'not being extraordinary' with 'a rough patch' and 'a rough patch' with 'everything' and 'everything' with 'all over the place'.

Ask yourself: is the person really talking about 'everything' and 'all'? Bring your attention to the combinations and exaggerations and you will be able to reveal the flaws in the logic. The person felt that 'everything' was 'all over the place' but it wasn't: lots of things were in order, except for their thinking, of course. And even if 'everything' was 'all over the place', would that prevent them from being extraordinary? I don't think so: I'm sure there has been many an extraordinary inventor with a messy laboratory.

The Speed of Belief-Building

Some beliefs can be built really quickly and relatively easily. Others can take a lifetime. Below is a simple scenario that shows just how quickly a belief can be formed.

It is a sunny day. I am in my garden, sitting back on the deckchair, looking at my fifteen-year-old son Cian. He can do some really cool back flips, somersaults and tumbles on the trampoline. I think, 'I would really like to be good at that.' So, I hop up from my chair and ask Cian to teach me. In I plunge like a clapping seal into the trampoline and, after brief instruction, I am ready to try.

[*The thought process is as follows:*]

- **I would really like to be good at that.**
- I will try it.
- Oops!
- Not to worry: I will try it again.
- Nope! No joy!
- Okay, one more time.
- No! Not my thing. **I am no good at that!**

I pull myself up from face down on the floor of the trampoline and take a look at Cian. He is looking my way, recording everything on his camcorder. His body is shaking and he struggles to hold the camera steady because he is laughing so much.

[*It is a combination of the value we place on the goal and the emotional consequences of trying that determines whether we will make another attempt. This determines the rate at which we succeed or give in! The thought process is as follows:*]

- Right! Begin again …
- Nope, I knew it! I am no good at this stuff!
- Probably pointless, but I'll give it another go …
- Damn it! I just *knew* it!
- One last time …
- Ah, here! What's the point?

'Hey, Cian, you can have the trampoline back now. I'm done with it. And delete that video!'

Key point
Believing you can do something and repeatedly trying to do it are two very different things. Even if people persist with an action, the underlying belief can just reinforce itself. At that point, they are simply continuing to prove themselves right again and again. So many people get caught in this cycle and are therefore unable to change.

How Beliefs Are Presented

Now we know how beliefs are formed. We have also identified the problems that arise because of the filters of deletion, distortion and generalisation. We see how all this is backed up by the God Complex. Now, we need to look at how beliefs are held up under scrutiny.

A useful technique is to track *backwards*. This process starts at the point where the belief is already formed and has been projected out into the world. Start by taking a belief. Then reveal how it has come about by repeatedly asking, 'Why do you say that?' Each 'why' will trigger a 'because'. It is not always verbalised but if you pay attention you will notice that it is there.

ASSERTION
(I am right.)
Our belief/opinion is stated as a fact.

JUSTIFICATION
(I am right because …)
We explain our reasons. Three are usually enough.

CLARIFICATION
(… which means I am right.)
We explain why the reasons mean our belief is a fact.

CONCLUSION
(Therefore I am right.)
We express the obvious and 'natural' arrival at our 'fact'.

A Presenting Belief

Let's take an example of how a belief can be presented. John is a fifty-year-old male. He grew up in the 1960s. Times were tough and John had to leave school early to go to work on the family farm. As a result, he developed a belief around school, particularly around maths.

Process	Circular Belief System	Underlying Premise
Assertion	I am no good at maths	I am right
Justification	**Because, because, because** I am no good at maths	Because I am right
Clarification	**Which means that** I am no good at maths	Which means that I am right
Conclusion	**Therefore** I am no good at maths	Therefore I am right

Here is the conversation as it took place in my practice:

John: I am no good at maths.

Brian: What makes you say that?

Once challenged, John delivers Justification 1.

John: **Because** I am no good with figures.

Brian: How do you know?

When challenged, John delivers Justification 2.

John: I know **because** I was never any good in school.

Brian: That was a long time ago and you were a different person then. Could you not give it another shot now that you are much older?

John consolidates his position with Justification 3.

John: There is no point **because** I wouldn't get any better at it.

Brian:	How can you be so sure?

At this point, John offers Clarification 1.

John:	Well, you see, it's just that I am not that type of person. Do you know **what I mean?**
Brian:	No.

John now offers Clarification 2.

John:	Some people are cut out for figures and stuff and some people aren't. *(That's what I mean.)*
Brian:	Really?

John is getting a bit fed up now, so he offers Clarification 3.

John:	Yeah, I struggle to put two and two together for God's sake, so don't start asking me about what is it called? Calculus? Theorems? Give us a break, will ya? I am not being smart or anything, Brian, but you are at nothing. You are wasting your time. It's not going to happen. Honestly! *(That's also what I mean.)*
Brian:	You think?

This is one question too many and John feels like it's a direct challenge. Now the emotions kick in. I have taken it too far and it's time for John to put me back in my place. The God Complex is at work here.

John:	I think? I think? Are you kidding me? I don't think it! I *know* it for a fact. I am just one of those people who's not good at that type of thing. I am no good at maths and there are no two ways about

> it! Maths and me just don't go together.
> Never did, never will – fact.

This is a good example of how a belief can be presented. At this point in the conversation with John, you'd be forgiven for wondering, 'Why bother?' Well, bothering to uncover beliefs can really help people and give them more options. Later in this chapter, I will give you a selection of sure-fire questions to challenge *any* belief and create movement.

A Word of Caution

It is obvious from the example of John and his beliefs surrounding maths, that you must be careful when questioning a person's beliefs. When you question a person's beliefs, you bring into question their sense of certainty about the world. Because of this, you are likely to provoke an emotional reaction. If you persist with your challenge, you are even more likely to produce a negative emotional response. So the tools you are learning here need to be used with *respect* and *tact*. It is not wise to challenge beliefs just because you can. Remember: just because it is not your belief does not mean that the belief is not working for the other person!

All belief-change work depends on getting prior permission. So, before you go challenging someone's beliefs, consider the fact that you are entering 'sacred space'. These beliefs can and often do represent *who* the person is and so a challenge to the belief is an affront to their identity. That can be destructive, so it is wise to be well versed in these skills before you go using them. If you want to start somewhere, start with *yourself*. Always keep in mind this maxim: 'Live and let live.' Everyone has their own formula for living, so please be respectful and compassionate; it will serve you well in the long run.

Let me give you an example that I often use in my seminars. At one such seminar, I had just explained the process of belief formation and change when one of the delegates raised his hand to ask a question. Kevin was a young man in his early twenties. He had blond hair, tanned skin and was tall, dark, extremely fit and a big hit with the ladies. He worked in a gym as a fitness instructor and nutrition adviser. His entire body radiated perfect health, so he was a living example of 'walking his talk'. Kevin had a concerned look on his face; he was obviously worried. Impressed by the noticeable potential in this process, he had in mind a situation where it could be used to great effect. The only problem was he was not sure if he had mastered the skills yet. So he asked me, 'Brian, would it be possible to use these skills anywhere?' I said, 'For example?' He replied, 'Well my mum and dad are getting on in years and their health really isn't good at all and I am worried for them. So would it be possible to get them to change their beliefs around their diet so that they would start eating healthily and have a better chance of living longer?'

Kevin's question was well-meaning. He loved his mum and dad and wanted them to be healthier. On the face of it, there is nothing wrong with that. However, the skills involved in challenging beliefs are really powerful and provocative. It is a questioned-based system and the nature of targeted questions is to produce doubt in the listener. If you do this without prior permission, that is an intrusion, a violation of the person's right to choose. There is also some projection involved here, in this case, Kevin's view of what he believed to be healthy or unhealthy. Now, my guess would be that Kevin was right – but this was leaving out the crucial element of choice. His parents were making choices every day. One of those choices was to eat how they wished. If they chose to change that, it would need to be their decision and not his. So I asked Kevin, 'Have you spoken to your parents about their eating habits?' He replied, 'Oh yes. I have been on to them for ages to change but they just won't listen!' I replied: 'Would it be fair to say that perhaps it is not that they won't listen, it may be that they choose differently? And isn't that their right?' Kevin wasn't too happy with the response but he understood the implications of his intended actions.

Pythagoras Theory

Did you know that Pythagoras, the Greek mathematician, believed that: you should never pick up something if you dropped it; you should never lay your hands on a white chicken; and you should never stir the fire with a poker? Pythagoras considered himself to be semi-divine and attracted a number of followers called 'Pythagoreans'. Pythagoreans believed that reality was mathematical in nature. So *one* was the number of reason, *two* the number of opinion, *three* the number of harmony, *four* the number of justice, *five* the number of marriage, etc.

Pythagoreans were also vegetarians. In fact, up until recently, a 'Pythagorean diet' was a common name for vegetarian. Curiously though, the Pythagorean code prohibited the consumption or even the touching of any sort of bean. Some said it was because they believed beans represented the soul; some said it was because beans resembled genitalia. Cicero, on the other hand, suggested that it was because beans produce farts. History has it that Pythagoras' aversion to beans actually cost him his life. Accounts of Pythagoras' murder state that, when his enemies set fire to his house, he tried to get away but ran in the direction of a bean field. He came to a sudden stop and declared that he would rather die than enter the field. So with that, his pursuers caught up with him, slit his throat and that was the end of it.

Questioning Beliefs

We have seen that you need to pay attention to how your beliefs are formed. As a rule of thumb, if the belief is not stopping you from doing anything, then leave it as it is. However, if a belief is holding you back, you can challenge it. Thanks to the exemplary work of Richard Bandler and John Grinder, we now have the capacity to use *targeted questions* that will challenge any belief.

In this section, I will show you exactly *where* the questions are targeted. This is useful to know but it is not essential. If all you do is become familiar with and learn these questions off by heart, you will manage to shake the foundation of any limiting belief. The questions we will use come from the Meta Model developed by Bandler and Grinder.

The Meta Model

The Meta Model is a set of questions specifically designed to challenge any limiting beliefs you may have. It does this by:
* Recovering missing information
* Challenging problematic meanings
* Introducing options.

It's now time to do a little language study! This won't take long. Keep in mind that this is language *as it affects the brain*, so it won't necessarily conform to standard English.

We will return to our opening belief but this time we will add more to it and then we will shift it with great precision.

> *How can I be extraordinary? I am going through a bit of a rough patch at the minute and everything is all over the place. I have to say that this is the worst one yet.*

Let's put it into a Meta Model.

Target	Description	Question(s)
Nouns	The people, places and things	Who, what, when, where, which, specifically?
Verbs	The actions, states and occurrences	How, specifically?
Generalisations	All, always, every, never, etc.	All, always, every, never?
Modal operators	Possibilities: can, is, will, am, like, want, wish, etc. Necessities: have to, ought, need, should, must, etc.	What stops you? What would happen if you could? What would it be like if…? Comparisons
Best, most, worst,	least, etc. Compared to who or	what?
Causes	This causes that	How does this cause that?
Meanings	This means that	How does this mean that?

It is not important where you begin, so long as you do. Every single question will provoke a response and engage the mind of the person you are questioning.

Some Principles to Keep In Mind

- Remember first and foremost, this can be an emotionally challenging journey for the subject.
- Make sure you have permission before doing this.
- You need to focus on the process of what they are saying, not the content.
- You can ask the same question as many times as needed.
- Stick with the questions and avoid offering advice.

- Expect excuses, contradictions, rejections, etc. This is the God Complex at work because they are feeling vulnerable and are trying to save face.
- If they change the definition of their belief, keep going.
- No need to stick with the opening statement. You can Meta Model each answer as it is presented to you; they are all connected to the belief.
- Do not expect the person to agree with your questions.
- Do not expect them to be altogether comfortable with them either.
- Avoid giving your own commentary on what is happening.
- Show compassion, as this will feel like an assault.
- Inject some humour if you can.
- Soften your tone of voice a little so that it does not sound threatening.
- Use 'softeners' when asking questions: 'I am curious', 'I was wondering', 'Could you possibly tell me?'
- Give the person time to respond.
- Allow them the time and space to arrive at their own conclusions.

> **Key point**
> Avoid using 'why?' when you challenge a *belief*. All it does is drive the person deeper into their justifications and strenghten their belief. Use 'why?' only when you are looking for *reasons*.

Now let's use the Meta Model to dissect the belief.

How can I be extraordinary? I am going through a bit of a rough patch at the minute and everything is all over the place. I have to say that this is the worst one yet.

Nouns	The people, places and things	Who, what, when, where, which, specifically?

- We know the *who* involved, so no need to ask that.
- *What* do you mean by 'extraordinary'?
- *What* do you mean by 'a bit'?
- *What* do you mean by 'a rough patch'?

- *What* do you mean by 'a bit of a rough patch'?
- *What* do you mean by 'all over the place'?

Verbs	The actions, states and occurrences	How, specifically?

- How, specifically, *can* you become extraordinary?
- How could you do that?
- How do you mean you are 'going' through a rough patch?
- How, specifically, *is* this the worst one yet?

Generalisations	All, always, every, never, etc.	All, always, every, never?

- Everything is all over the place?
- Every single thing? There is not one single thing in place?
- All over the place?
- All? You mean absolutely everywhere?

Modal operators	Possibilities: can, is, will, am, like, want, wish, etc. Necessities: have to, ought, need, should, must, etc.	What stops you? What would happen if you could? What would it be like if…?

- What stops you from being extraordinary?
- What would happen if you could be extraordinary?
- What would it be like if you could ?

Comparisons	Best, most, worst, least, etc.	Compared to who or what?

- The worst one yet compared to what?

Causes	This causes that	How does this cause that?

- How does the fact that you are going through a bit of a rough patch cause you to believe that you can't be extraordinary?

Meanings	This means that	How does this mean that?

- How does the fact that you are going through a bit of a rough patch mean that you can't be extraordinary?

You can see that there is a stack of questions on the list. There is no getting away from them. Each question will offer up new information, add new perspectives and give the subject more choices. In short, it will expand their map of the world. This is a very thorough system; it needs to be.

Exercise: Question Your Belief

Question one of your own beliefs by using the Meta Model, following the format below. Write your answers in the chart – and then use the Meta Model on them, too!

'It's unrealistic to expect me to move from being ordinary to becoming extraordinary.'	Answer
Who says?	
What do you mean by 'realistic'?	
How do you know I am being unrealistic?	
How do you know you can't become extraordinary?	
How do you mean 'move'?	
Has no one ever done it before?	
Can no one become extraordinary? Ever?	
What stops you?	
What would happen if you could?	
What do you mean by 'extraordinary'?	
What do you mean by 'ordinary'?	

Exercise: Question Your Negative Beliefs

This may be one of the most powerful exercises you ever do. Write down all the negative things that you say to yourself about yourself: the things that go through your head when you mess up, make a mistake or think you can't do something.

Most people give themselves a hard time. Most people are on their own case a lot! Typical negative commentary could be:

There you go; you're an awful muppet! Making a fool of yourself again. What are you like? You will never be able to do that! What will people think? They are all waiting for you to fall flat on your face, you know. Nobody will believe you. They'll all criticise you! You really are stupid.

Sound familiar? Now write all the negative things you say to yourself.

Now call yourself on it! Take each statement and run it through the questions. No indulging yourself: keep asking the questions. If you get stuck, move to another statement and come back to it later. If you still can't figure it out, just think about what the solution would look like and commit to concentrating on that. These are the things to ask:

- Who? What? When? Where? Which?
- Who says?
- How do you know?
- What do you mean?
- What stops you?
- What would happen if you could?
- Always? Every? Never?
- Compared to who or what?
- How does *this* cause *that*?
- How does *this* mean *that*?

When you have finished this exercise, I recommend you set aside some time to listen to the *Mind of Genius* CD that accompanies this book.

CHAPTER 9

Mind Your Language

*One day I sat thinking, almost in despair; a hand fell on my shoulder
and a voice said reassuringly: cheer up, things could get worse.
So I cheered up and, sure enough, things got worse.*

James Hagerty

PMA, Positive Mental Attitude: I expect you have heard the phrase being used before; maybe you have used it yourself once or twice. If you are like the rest of us, you have probably tried it out without really knowing what it is all about. PMA involves holding an optimistic outlook on every situation no matter how bad, with the view that if you look for the positive, you bring about the positive. The concept was put into mainstream consciousness via Napoleon Hill's excellent book *Think and Grow Rich*. Funnily enough, the statement in the title was never actually used in the book. Of course, Sherlock Holmes never actually said, 'Elementary, my dear Watson.' And Captain Spock never said, 'It's life, Jim, but not as we know it.'

The PMA concept has become a little dated and, in a sense, has been replaced by the Law of Attraction, which came from Rhonda Byrne's book *The Secret*. Both ideas are essentially the same and both are really useful concepts. The Law of Attraction operates on a higher level of efficiency and requires only that you be grateful for what you want. It asks that you behave in a manner as if you already have whatever it is you want; in doing this, it will come to you. PMA emphasises the importance of self-talk as a way of promoting a healthy state of mind that will inevitably bring about your success in life. It goes on to suggest the use of positive affirmations. The principle being that if you state what you want and keep affirming that mentally, several times every day, then you will bring it into your life. So if you want to be healthy, wealthy and wise, all you need to do is to keep saying it over and over again, until your mind gets the message and makes you do it. It is a simple idea and a nice idea; but it is not an idea that works for everyone. Having said that, the underlying principle of the idea is useful.

The quality of your self-talk determines the results you get in life but it is not just *what* you say to yourself that counts; it is *how* you say what you say that makes the difference. We know from the earlier chapter that the beliefs you hold can be either limiting or empowering. They act as fences around your potential. So if you don't believe you can do something, then no amount of self-talk will change that.

If you really want to adopt a PMA, you need to consider three things: your feelings, your existing belief system and the content and quality of your self-talk.

> **The Three Keys to PMA:**
> - **Your Feelings**
> - **Your Beliefs**
> - **Your Self-Talk.**

Getting this combination right will make extraordinary things happen in your life. All three concepts are interrelated. Your beliefs produce your self-talk; and your self-talk impacts on your feelings. If you want to bring about a profound change in your thinking and raise things up a level, you need to know how to talk to yourself in a manner that works. In fact, you need to become your own personal hypnotist!

Before you learn how to do that, let's take a step back and examine how our beliefs are formed in the first instance. If we know how a belief is built, that means we can go about building some of our own without waiting for circumstance or life experiences to be the causative factor. Interestingly, the best place to start working on this skill set is *not* on you but on *others*. This is because language is better understood when it is externalised and targeted at someone else.

In Chapter 8, we examined the three filters: Deletion, Distortion and Generalisation. These are the operations that occur in the mind and lead to us creating beliefs. In summary, we pay selective attention to certain things around us (deletion). Then we label these events and experiences and in so doing we alter their meaning (distortion). Finally, we make assumptions based on what we have paid attention to and created meaning for (generalisation). Therefore, if you want to build your own set of beliefs you will need to *mirror this process*.

We already know that the three filters cause our assumptions to be flawed. However, that doesn't stop us from projecting our assumptions and beliefs out into the world. When we do, we are liable to make another false assumption by thinking that what is true for us must be true for everyone else.

Mind Reading 101

I say, 'Life is good!' When I say this, it is because I have found this to be true for me. In making this statement, I suggest that what is good for the goose is good for the gander. If it is true for me, that means that it must be true for you. Thinking otherwise might shake the foundations of my assumptions. Therefore, if you challenge me I am likely to *tell you why* it is good and not take on board your perspective. We are guilty of doing this all the time. Life is projection. 'Everything is a mirror', 'You get out of life what you put into it', 'People are good', 'Things can change': all of these statements are projections of my own world view, but each one is technically a Mind Read. I am suggesting that these are universal truths and it may be that you do not see them that way, but they are 'true'. I am emotionally invested in what I am saying so I want you to agree with me. I have already put the keys in my hypnosis machine.

Other *mind reads* are a lot more obvious. Think of this common phrase: 'Do you know what I mean?' This is a mind read. How do I know that you know what I mean? This is not really a check for understanding; it is a check for *agreement*. When I use this phrase, I am expecting you to agree with 'the truths' I have constructed that are self-evident to me. I can take this further by saying, '**I realise** that you will need to think about this some more and **I am aware** that this may all be new to you but **you may be wondering** when **you will get to understand** it, but you will when you **think it through**.' This sentence contains multiple mind reads. Of course, if I am right about these mind reads, you are more likely to accept what I am saying to you. This is where my outward projection becomes something more; in fact, it becomes an installation. I take my world view and impose it on you through my words.

The bad news: this is happening all of the time. The good news: everyone is doing it. The even better news: if you learn how to do it really well you can improve your own life and the lives of others to extraordinary degrees. The warning: be careful of your own press. Remember: you could be wrong!

The Power of 'You'

Projection happens automatically. We do it without even thinking about it. We speak and, as we do, we weave our hypnotic webs around each other, shaping, influencing and steering each other's minds in various directions. But what if I want to influence you deliberately? If I want to put a thought inside your head intentionally, I can. If I work to the same formula that you use when building your own beliefs, not only can I put in a thought or an idea, I can build an entire belief system.

My son Cian makes movies; and one of his key skills is his ability to create a first person view. This draws you into each scene and gives you an idea of what it would be like to be there. All great movies do that. They invite you into the scene by presenting it in a certain way and by making you empathise with the actors, the script or both. This is the art used in great storytelling. The way it is done in *language* is by a simple change in reference. Notice the difference in the following descriptions.

From 'I'

'Yesterday I went to an ACDC gig. It was great fun. There was a big crowd there. They were really into it. It was very good. The band played really well. They were very loud. I was in the mosh-pit for a lot of it. I was very close to the stage right beside the speakers. I was wrecked after it but one of my friends handed me a can of Coke. That was deadly. I drank it. It was lovely.'

To 'You'

'Yesterday I went to see ACDC. Now, I don't know whether you like them or not, but have you ever been to a gig where the crowd is going mental and you are right there in the thick of it? The music is blasting out through the speakers, you're having a great time, singing and dancing your heart out to the music. You know when you know all the words and the band are just really into it? You've got the whole air-guitar thing going on and everything! You are that close that you could nearly step onto the stage. Well, it was one of those types of gigs. I was soaked to the skin, the sweat was pouring off me. You know how it is: standing there still buzzing from the craic. You feel fantastic and whacked at the same time and someone hands you a lovely, cold can of Coke. Oh man, it was deadly!'

Preframing

Storytelling is powerful. Changing the reference from 'I' to 'you' is very effective. Another technique that is very powerful is your ability to set up a person's perspective of something in advance. For example, if I tell you a happy story well enough, you get to be happy. If I tell you a sad story, well, you know how it goes.

What if I say to you before you meet someone, that you would want to keep an eye on them? That there is something 'not quite right' about them? Now, you know your own mind, don't you? And you will make up your own mind, won't you? But let me ask you this: when you do meet that person, are you not making up your own mind as to whether you need to keep an eye on them or not? This means that already my statement has directed your thinking. Your initial thoughts are a reflection and a reaction to what I have said to you previously. In the world of NLP, there is a name for this: it is called Preframing. It is wise to keep an eye on the intentions behind what people are saying about keeping an eye on people, if you get my meaning ...

Would the Real Healer Please Stand Up?

If you have ever been to an effective mind coach or hypnotherapist, this is what they do: they do not heal you but they do teach you how to tap into your own healing abilities. If you have ever attended an effective mind coach or hypnotherapist and your goal was *not* achieved, the thing that probably prevented it was your belief in either your ability to change or in the coach or therapist's ability to change you. The truth of the matter is that you cannot change without your own consent. The next time you hear a mind coach or therapist tell you that they can heal you, be wary. If they claim they can, they are either misguided, ill-informed or downright dishonest.

People come to me all the time looking to be healed. I get clients from all over Europe who have heard me on the radio, seen me on TV or online, read my book, attended a seminar or heard it through the grapevine. Many of them expect me to heal them. I tell them I can't heal anybody – I am not a healer – but I can teach them the skills and create the environment where they get to make the changes they want and achieve the goals that they are looking for. I am not healing them: I am simply tapping into their own abilities. I am helping them to use their brains more effectively and one of the key ways that I do that is through the use of my *language*.

When it works, it is down to three elementary principles. One: I have created a rapport with the client; two: the client wants to change; and three: I know how to transfer the skills required for that. That's it! Nothing more; nothing less. No magic wands, no voodoo, no swinging watches: just those three simple things. It's simple, but those three things combined are hugely powerful and transformative.

The Three Not-so-stunningly-amazing 'Secrets' to Effective Changework

1. There needs to be rapport between the client and the changeworker.

2. The client needs to want to change.

3. The changeworker needs to know how to transfer the skills to the client.

What The Hypnotists Don't Want You To Know

All language is hypnotic. Every communication contains suggestion. You are being programmed every time you hear a word. Those words could be your own, they could be mine or they could belong to someone else. Words direct consciousness. As you are reading this text, your consciousness is being directed. Therefore, my words are determining your thinking. If you are running an internal commentary as you read what I have written, then you are controlling your thinking – but only in the moment that you commenting. As soon as your attention returns to the text, then I have the reins again. Yes, you have given me permission and for that I am genuinely grateful and privileged – thank you – but nonetheless, you have handed over your attention; in doing that, you are opening up to the effect of my influence. That may appear obvious to you. However, can I ask you to stop for a moment and think about the consequences of that? What people are given permission to influence your thinking every single day? You switch on the news and your attention is guided by the newsreader to misery and mayhem, but you need to know what's happening in the world. Isn't that why they say he who controls the media controls the message? *Whoever has your attention is the one that is guiding your thinking.*

But that's life – and we love to be affected by it. We watch a movie and we let ourselves be affected emotionally. We meet a friend, they tell us a story and we love being affected by it. We speak to one another every day and we are affected by it. You are reading this book and you are being affected by it – in the most positively empowering ways, I hope! In our minds, we see this as normal; and it is. We believe that we are in control and we are, to an extent: the extent to what we choose to pay attention to. As you read these words, ask yourself who you are listening to most: you or me? You could be listening to both of us in equal measure but that is precisely the point. In order for you to read one word, you need to hand over your attention. Think of the town criers of old, who rang their bells in the town square and hollered, 'Ladies and gentlemen, lend me your ears!' They would have been more accurate in saying, 'Lend me your *minds*!'

How to Install a Credible Belief

The fact that words are hypnotic and human beings use them to speak means that human beings are hypnotic, too. Every word you speak affects and directs the thinking of others. But it also affects you. You are also an audience for what you say. It affects you as much, if not more. Every word and sentence leads you either towards limitation or possibility. Every word produces a response inside of you and every response determines what you do. Any storyteller will say, 'It's not what you tell them, it's the way you tell them.' This is particularly true of your internal self-talk. By the end of this chapter, I expect you will really see the value of what I am suggesting and you will begin to harness the reins of your internal dialogue so that you can begin the process of building a more beautiful mind.

To learn how powerful language really is, let's look at how we project our ideas and beliefs on the world. Once our belief is formed, we project it out into the world as a fact. We make our assertions and we are ready, if required, to back them up with clarifications and justifications. I say, 'Life is good!' You ask, 'What makes you say that?' I say, 'Because the sun is shining, the day is young and it's the weekend!' In one sentence I have given you my justifications and clarifications. Let's break down what happened.

The Belief	The Assumptions	The 'Facts'
Life is good	I am right about this	Because all of the evidence says so
	Because this is true	The sun is shining
	Because this is true	The day is young
	Because this is true	It's the weekend
	Which means that	Life is good

The simple truth is that I get to believe that 'life is good' based on my experience or knowledge. My experience and knowledge are facts and you can't dispute the facts. If you do, I will just defend them.

What's very interesting is the way in which we add up the facts. Lewis Carroll, of *Alice in Wonderland* fame, makes this exact point in his poem, 'The Hunting of the Snark'.

The Hunting of the Snark
Fit the First
The Landing

'Just the place for a Snark!' the Bellman cried,
As he landed his crew with care;
Supporting each man on the top of the tide
By a finger entwined in his hair.

'Just the place for a Snark! I have said it twice:
That alone should encourage the crew.
Just the place for a Snark! I have said it thrice:
What I tell you three times is true.'

The *rule of three* is a format you will often hear in speeches by politicians and orators. This is because of its persuasive power. Human beings like things being grouped into threes: Father, Son and Holy Spirit; *The Good, the Bad and the Ugly*; 'government of the people, by the people and for the people'. When it comes to belief-building, we also like the rule of three. If you take another look at the belief above, you will see that it conforms to the rule of three. 'Life is good' because *this* is true, and *this* is true, and *this* is true. If *this* is true, and *this* is true, and *this* is true, then my belief must be true. In the world of business, these are called 'yes sets' (though I've rarely heard them used properly there).

When we take this tendency into account and combine it with the skills of rapport, we now have the tools to set about building and installing a belief in someone else. What you need to do then is *pace your method of gathering evidence* and arriving at conclusions. This is how it can work:

'Hi, my name is Brian.' *(Slight pause.)*

'Brian Colbert.' *(Slight pause.)*

'And I am a Master Trainer of NLP.' *(Slight pause.)*

'And what I want to do today is to teach you how you can use NLP to help you to learn more effectively.'

In NLP, the first three statements are called Truisms. Truisms are things that are easily verifiable and not open to challenge. I say, 'You are reading this sentence.' That is a truism. If I say *three* things that you can immediately verify (or don't feel the need to verify), you become more open to what I am about to say next.

Do you see how this has worked? I say, 'Hi, my name is Brian.' You are unlikely to challenge that; instead you agree. You may do that with a head nod, an external 'yes' or an internal affirmation ('yeah', 'aha' or 'hmm'). Then I follow on from there and say, 'Brian Colbert.' You repeat the process for a second time. Then, on the third round, I say, 'And I am a Master Trainer of NLP.' You are likely to agree with that statement, too. At this stage, I am beginning to establish an agreement frame with you. Therefore, when I throw in the next statement (provided that it is not too far removed from my first set of statements), it is likely to get accepted by you as a matter of fact. All I have done is let you see that *this* is true, and *this* is true, and *this* is true; and then I let you do the rest by making the natural leap that you normally make when creating assumptions. You suggest to yourself, 'Well, if *this* is true, and *that* is true, and *that* is true, then it follows that what he has just said is true.'

In actual fact, I may *not* be able to do what I am suggesting. Of course, in reality, *I can* and you know that I can because I have written two books and I am a certified hypno/psychotherapist and I have been training this stuff for years, so I'm obviously a total and complete awesome legend of a genius! Now, do you see what's happening in this last statement? I used the truisms again but this time I made a *leap too far*. This is how it worked. I said 'you know that I can because':

> 'I have written two books' *(True.)*
> 'I am a certified hypno/psychotherapist' *(True.)*
> 'I have been training this stuff for years' *(True.)*

Then I made a leap too far:

> 'I'm obviously a total and complete awesome legend of a genius!'

Because this is a leap too far, you are likely to question, dismiss or laugh at that statement. In that moment, I broke the rapport. I broke the flow and, in doing so, I lost the connection and the ability to influence.

Of course, I could get back on track. I could say:

> 'Only kidding! Actually, one of the things about hypnosis is that a lot of people are using it to learn how to relax.' *(True.)*

I could progress this with:

> 'Even the British NHS has approved it as an acceptable form of treatment.' *(True. You may not have known this already but you are likely to agree.)*

I could then say:

> 'And Irish doctors are being advised to examine these complementary alternatives.' *(Again, you are likely to agree.)*

> 'So, in fact, it is something that is at least worth having a closer look at for yourself.' *(Since this is not too much of a stretch, you are likely to hear me out.)*

How to Set Up an Agreement Frame

1. Create *rapport* on as many levels as possible.
2. Use the *rule of three*.
3. Use *truisms*.
4. Add in suggestion at the end.
5. Repeat.
6. Start small and gradually increase the amount of suggestions.
7. Tap into the power of emotions.

The Devil is in the Detail

We have examined the *process* of installing a credible belief, which is hugely effective. But the real magic lies in the finer nuances of language. When it comes to your ability to transfer your ideas into another person's mind, the devil really is in the detail – and opportunity is in the lack of it! The tools I draw on here were first demonstrated by renowned hypnotherapist Milton Erickson and later incorporated into NLP. The key to effective persuasion lies in your ability to be able to pace a person's reality, and then propose a more useful alternative.

In Chapter 8, we examined how to challenge beliefs through the use of persistent questioning. Here, we look at another approach, one that is all about being *deliberately vague*. In using questions, the aim is for something to be specified; using a *lack of detail*, you force the person to go inside their own mind and create their own meaning. Here's how it might work. You say:

'Things are getting me down.'

I don't challenge this belief with lots of questions. I say:

'Won't it be great when they begin to look up again?'
or
'Let's take a look at the situation so you can get a handle on it.'
or
'Why not take a break and that will give you lift?'

If you examine what I have said, it's clear that I have not given any real detail about how to help or how to resolve the issue. It just appears like I have; and my statements make the other person think about what I have said.

Let's work through a more detailed example. A person says:

'Life is crap.'

You are unlikely to change their view if you say, 'No it's not – it's great.' If you want to help them out of that prison you need to use the right keys. You need to first set up the Agreement Frame and remember the three keys to effective change: rapport, permission and skill. You also need to take into account how their feelings and self-talk are impacting on their belief. Remember: when they say that 'life is crap', they are saying that out of certainty; so you need to respect that. First, just try to get them on board. You could say:

So you feel that life is crap at the moment. I guess there must be a lot of things going wrong and you haven't been able to get through them, or things are not working out right and you need to get a handle on them. Hopefully, like all things, you will find a way to get through and to sort it out. And maybe if you do, you will begin to see things in a different light and come up with some ways that will help.

What I have done here is present my response in a way that does not contradict or directly challenge what the other person has said. However, while I was responding, I started a process of suggestion. I began deliberately putting ideas into the other person's mind. This is all subtly done and for the most part will go unnoticed by the other person. I did this by inserting vague suggestions about how they could overcome this problem or perspective. The purpose of being vague is to allow me to keep a level of rapport with them and also to allow them to make sense of what I am saying in a way that means something to them. Remember: my intention is to *help*; to do anything else would be immoral.

I did this mainly by **embedding commands** in my sentences.

Embedded Commands

Your conscious mind is your first line of defence. We often refer to it as the critical mind. It is the mind that asks all the questions. It is there to help you filter incoming information and to prevent you from paying attention to or responding to irrelevant stuff.

However, it can be bypassed. The way it can be bypassed is through *repetitive suggestion*. To get past the critical mind, a connection needs to be built, based on the principles I mentioned earlier. Once the connection is established, suggestions can be installed through a process called *analogue marking* and *embedding commands*. The thoughts, words and suggestions that you want the subconscious mind to get to work on are emphasised by using a slightly deeper inflection in your intonation than you normally use. In this way, the deeper mind gets the message and begins to act on it.

Your results will depend on the number of suggestions you give, whether you have rapport or not, and your level of skill. When your suggestions are embedded in larger sentences, they are less likely to be resisted, since the overall sentences appear as if you are just making a comment rather than demanding that person does something. Suggestion strengthens upon repetition and this is fundamental to success.

Let's go back to the example to see how embedded commands might work there. In the text below, I have highlighted the embedded commands.

So you feel that life is crap at the moment. I guess there must be a lot of things going wrong and you haven't been able to **get through them**, or things are not working out right and you need to **get a handle on them**. Hopefully, like all things, you will **find a way to get through** and to **sort it out**. And maybe if you do, you will **begin to see things in a different light** and **come up with some ways that will help**.

There are more hidden suggestions in there, but can you see how different that response is from how it first appeared? It would be naive to expect that one sentence like that would change that person's mindset completely; but what it does manage, is to keep the rapport going and begin building the foundation for change. Can you imagine a full two-hour discussion around that? Can you consider the amount of suggestions that would be created in the direction of a positive result? Now imagine that process being combined with the questioning technique in Chapter 8 and you will begin to appreciate the power of the skills that you are learning here.

Negative Commands

If I say, '**Do not bother** trying to master these skills straight away', I have already set your mind up yet again. One of the things we know about the subconscious mind is that it can't process a negative. So if I say, '**Do not think** about being extraordinary', for your mind to understand it you have to think (if only for a moment) about being extraordinary. Each time you think about it, you increase the possibility of it happening.

For example, notice the mix here, there are embedded commands *and* negative commands being used at the one time.

> This book is designed to help you to **live an exceptional life**. Now I am **not expecting** that you **go and make every day extraordinary**. I just want you to **have more extraordinary days**. To me, it is **not important** that you **focus on this at every opportunity that you get**. What is important is that you **focus on it more often**. Do you know what I mean?

Now think about those school teachers who inadvertently create a struggle ahead of time:

> Ok, ok, keep it down! Right, welcome to fifth year maths. Now, I know some of **you will struggle** this year and if you **act the maggot, you will fail**. But **I am not here to make things difficult for you. Maths is not all that bad**, so if you **knuckle down** you should**n't fall flat on your faces and fail**.

Embedded Questions

I wonder **can you see now how important it is to pay attention to how you talk to yourself?** I am also curious whether you will **begin to make good use of this information**. Right now I am asking myself, will you **take this stuff on board and make your life so much better** because of it? Do you **get the idea**? Commands can be embedded inside questions, too!

Presuppositions

Commands, whether they are direct or indirect, go to the heart of the matter and their focus is on the action that you want to happen. What I want to do now is to play around with the way a command or an idea can be interpreted. There is plenty of scope in language to imply things and to strengthen or soften words or even colour their meaning. In NLP, we call these Presuppositions. A presupposition, like a belief, is an assumption. A presupposition assumes what has to be present for something to make sense or be true. It takes certain things to be self-evident. Here are some examples:

Who read this book?

What is assumed here is that there is a book, there is a person and that they can read. That's all the stuff you take for granted but it wasn't all stated in the sentence. It is assumed to be obvious.

John read this book – and loved it, too.

What are the assumptions here? John exists, he can read, the book exists, he loves it and someone else loves it, too. Notice how 'too' could mean 'you, too' or not; that is deliberate.

Fortunately, John read this book and another great one like it.

This is pushing things even further. The above statement is moving beyond the facts and starting to colour what is being said with the intention of having it better received. If you say 'fortunately', it determines that everything that follows is good. When you add in 'another great one like it', that suggests that this book is also great. So now what you have got is: it is fortunate and great to read the book.

When presuppositions are stacked together, they gain more strength.

Fortunately, John could easily read and understand this delightful, life-changing book – and a few more of the great classics, too, like Dale Carnegie's *How to Win Friends and Influence People*.

Now we have really pushed the boat out. At this stage, all of these things are being assumed:
- It is fortunate to read the book.
- The book is a delight to read.
- It is easy to read and understand.
- It is a life-changing book.
- It is a great book.
- It is a classic.

The way presuppositions work is that the more there are, the harder it is to avoid accepting them. Let's take the last example and imagine that your response to it is: 'That's a bit of a push now, Brian; it's hardly a classic!' In saying this, you are still accepting the likelihood that it is easy to read and understand, that it is a delight, etc. Can you see how that operates?

Negative presuppositions work, too. I could just as easily have said, 'Unfortunately, the book is difficult to read and complicated to understand ', etc.

Politicians are forever using presuppositions; badly, I might add. Often they will get the hang of one and use it to death! Next time you tune in to an interview with a politician, listen out for their opening sentences. They start with things like: 'clearly', 'obviously', 'going forward', etc. These are all presuppositions.

Time Presuppositions
Time presuppositions include: 'before', 'after', 'during', 'as', 'when', 'while', 'begin', 'stop', 'start', 'yet', 'already', etc. Here's an example of them at work:

Before I begin to explain what I mean by the word presupposition, I want you to stop for a while and think about what you already know.'

It is assumed that I am going to explain, you are going to think about it, and you already know something.

Number Presuppositions

Number presuppositions include: 'first', 'second', 'last', 'another', etc. Here's an example of them at work:

> The first thing I want to speak to you about in becoming extraordinary is that you need only to do these few things and you will get there.

It is assumed that there is more than one thing I want to speak to you about, you will become extraordinary, etc.

Awareness Presuppositions

Awareness presuppositions include: 'realise', 'aware', 'know', 'notice', 'understand', etc. Here's an example of them at work:

> The fact that you are reading this means that you are already aware of the importance of learning; and it may just be that you don't realise it yet.

It is assumed that you are reading, you are learning and you will realise the importance of both.

Adverb Presuppositions

Adverb presuppositions include: 'deeply', 'easily', 'naturally', 'spontaneously', etc. Here's an example of them at work:

> I know that over time you will discover how easily you have absorbed this information and how naturally you will be speaking it every day.

It is assumed is that you have absorbed it and you will be speaking it every day.

Commentary Presuppositions

Commentary presuppositions include: 'clearly', 'obviously', 'fortunately', 'luckily', etc. Here is an example of them at work:

> Clearly, you are the type of person who deserves only the best that life can give; and, obviously, because of your stunning intellect and amazing abilities it is well within your reach. Naturally, you have the

passion and drive to go for it; so, fortunately, this will happen a lot more quickly than you may expect.

It is assumed that there is a type of person who deserves only the best, that you are this type of person, that you have a stunning intellect, etc.

Comparison Presuppositions

Comparison presuppositions include: 'nicer', 'better', 'happier', 'funnier', 'more', 'less', etc. Here is an example of them at work:

> Life is a lot sweeter when you allow yourself to be happier by looking at the funnier side of things.

It is assumed that life is sweet, that you are already happy in some way, and that there is a funny side to life.

Bringing It All Together Easily

Obviously, once you have read this chapter, you may well consider reading it another couple of times. Fortunately, each time that you do, it will make much more sense to you, as you find yourself really getting to grips with the content of it. I don't know whether you have realised it yet or not, but you can find all of these patterns in your everyday speech. So, really, you are not learning anything new at all; instead you are just highlighting stuff in a different way. The best thing about that is, when you do, you can make things so much better. I am not asking you to study these patterns: the first thing I am asking you to do is to play with them whenever you get the chance. Now I wonder can you imagine for me how good you will feel when you see the powerfully positive benefits that this knowledge will bring to you? The last thing I ask of you in relation to this is just to stay curious and know that it is not important how many you notice in one conversation or encounter. Clearly, if you notice any at all, you are already improving!

Now you have an idea how you can apply this to others, but how do you apply this to yourself? This is the fun bit! The beauty in this is that you can decide from now to allow yourself to use vague language on yourself more of the time. If you are facing a problem that you haven't figured out, or if you are facing a challenge that you really want to overcome, then you can begin to use the vague language suggestions to help your deeper mind come up with solutions.

Moving from Problem Frame to Solution Frame

The following example shows the process involved in moving from Problem Frame to Solution Frame. Let's start with a statement:

> I don't have a clue what to do. I won't be able to fix that. I am in trouble now. I will never get it sorted.

Imagine this running as a commentary in your head. This is the type of thing that happens when we are under pressure or anxious. When a problem is on your mind, your mind seems to repeat a handful of statements over and over again. So, as soon as you hear yourself, you need to take action. First, change your tone of voice at the crucial points. Get the commands moving, so your deeper mind takes them on board.

> I don't **have a clue what to do.** I won't **be able to fix that.** I am in trouble now. I will never **get it sorted.**

This will remind you to take control. When you do, add to the commentary. Pace it, so you are not deluding yourself, then do the additions.

> I wonder what it could look like when I **get it sorted.** Can I **imagine** what **the solution** could look like? How much better will I feel if I **figure this out?** What would happen if it all got to **be easier?** Fortunately, I know now how to program my deeper mind to **come up with the effective solutions** as quickly as possible.

Exercise: Problem Frame to Solution Frame

Think about something that has been causing you difficulty. Use the chart to guide yourself from Problem Frame to Solution Frame.

Statement
I will never be able to become extraordinary. I just don't have what it takes to be that sort of person.
Statement with Commands Highlighted
I will never **be able to become extraordinary**. I just don't **have what it takes** to **be that sort of person**.
Solutions
• Be able to be extraordinary. • Have what it takes. • Be that sort of person.
Solutions with Presuppositions
• I wonder if I could...be able to be extraordinary. • How much better will it feel if I...have what it takes. • How effective would it be to...be that sort of person.

1. Make a statement about your problem.
2. Use a highlighter to mark out any potential **commands** in the statement. These commands must be able to offer a solution.
3. Write out your solution.
4. Complete your solution with **presuppositions**.

As you complete this exercise, you will find your emotional state changing for the better. In itself, that will help you to think more clearly; and while you are building your PMA, why not invoke the Law of Attraction by expressing gratitude in advance for what your amazing, deep mind is about to do for you?

CHAPTER 10

The Stages of Life

No matter how bad things get, you got to go on living,
even if it kills you.

Sholom Aleichem

On 2 March 2012, the author and conservationist Lawrence Anthony passed into spirit. He was known internationally as the 'Elephant Whisperer'. His death did not go unnoticed. For almost twelve hours, two herds of wild South African elephants slowly, independently made their way through the Zululand bush until they reached Anthony's home. These formerly violent elephants were previously seen as pests and were destined to be shot; but they had been rescued and rehabilitated by Anthony, who had grown up in the bush. For two days, the herds stayed in Anthony's rural compound on the Thula Thula game reserve in the South African KwaZulu-Natal. They wanted to say goodbye to the man they loved. How they even knew of his death remains a mystery. Anthony was certainly a man who led an extraordinary life. Can you imagine how one person could make such a powerful impact that even their passing could result in the occurrence of such a phenomenal event? What you can do with the life that you have been gifted has yet to be fully scripted! Of course, it is rightfully down to your own design and interest. However, I think it is always worthwhile taking a look at what is possible *before* you make up your mind on it. I am not talking about recognition and fanfare; I am talking about impact and possibility.

In NLP, there is a profound question that I heard first from John La Valle: *What would you do if you knew you could?* As a mind coach, I often work with people on creating a life plan. Few people think through their life in any great detail. In general, they operate short- to medium-term. Ironically, as we get older and the time remaining gets shorter, we tend to start thinking long-term. We even think beyond our passing; morbid,

I know, but there you go. It took me until my late thirties before I even considered my mortality; and when I did, it lay the groundwork for a great big whopping mid-life crisis! That sent me into a tail-spin, for sure. But all of life's traumatic transitions carry with them profound learnings and powerful shifts in the nature of consciousness. Preparing for these eventualities is a tall order. I hardly expect that, even if I knew I was in for a mid-life crisis, I would've been able to ward it off. However, being able to recognise it may have saved me all the months I spent in denial.

I spent so much time questioning my ability to lift my general emotional state that I forgot to actually take heed of what the state was signalling. Mid-life crisis was not for me: I was *way* too together for that stuff! None of this big cars and fancy women nonsense. I have never lived mainstream, so why should I get a mainstream condition? I was intolerant of depression – just in myself, mind you. I held myself in 'higher' regard. I didn't do that type of a thing. I have always considered myself to be strong and capable of dealing with whatever life could throw at me. But mortality and old age well, I had a big problem with that. What then about the power of the mind? I have always had a great faith in that, too. But then there was this persistent nagging, hovering in the background. Every time I looked in the mirror, I could see I was being face-slapped by gravity and I wasn't bouncing back. I was able to deal with the times in my thirties when there was a noticeable shift in my energy. I was able to handle that through steely grit and unstoppable determination. I don't like to be pushed around by anyone – not even life itself.

So there I am, slap-bang in the middle of a losing battle and I have already decided that logic will not prevail. I am now starting to understand and sympathise with those scenes in the movies where the old guy tries running up the hill and his wife looks on hopelessly and says, 'He still thinks he is a young man.' I don't think we men are good at adjusting to this type of stuff. In my experience, women don't like it one bit either; but they just seem to get on with it. No tantrums, no big scenes, no iconic displays (well, maybe a few bad hair days every so often) but nothing compared to the scenes that we want to make.

Where did I end up? I found myself on the other side of the world; in Bahia, Brazil, just beside the Atlantic Ocean and on the edge of the Amazon jungle. I don't like creepy crawlies, I don't see the point of snakes and I hate lizards. What a way to go! Interestingly, after a few cups of Ayahuasca, it wasn't the spider monkeys, centipedes, giant grasshoppers, mosquitoes or pitch-black darkness of the jungle that concerned me. It was the fact that I had no longer had control of my mind. My mind went on this seven-hour trip, during which I experienced my entire life all over again. Every single event, significant or insignificant, was replayed at lightning speed, all of this happening alongside abstract imagery. I could see slimy serpents squirming in and out of my body, changing colour as they did ... all in a day's work! Go, team Brian! I can be an awful cabbage at times ...

Despite all the fuss and frolics, I made it through. I brought back with me much-needed insights and a deeper sense of connection with nature. My life has since been even more full because I see and appreciate it all a bit more. While I am still not happy with the pending outcome, I have settled for avoidance rather than denial. And I vow that I will ward off the grim reaper with every last breath, so to speak.

Whatever stage of life you are at now, there is always scope for improvement. That is the nature of evolution. But we all know each stage presents its own challenges and rewards. A little preparation could go a long way. There is a quote by François de La Rochefoucauld that fits with my opinion: 'We come fresh to the different stages of life, and in each of them we are usually quite inexperienced, no matter how old we are.' Inexperienced as we may be, there is no harm in being prepared. How about a plan for the eventuality, so that at least when we face the challenge, we know what it is we are facing? In that way, it can help us to integrate it, learn from it and even slay it. That is what is needed.

The definitions of life stages that feature in this chapter are loosely based on the work of distinguished people such as Erik Erikson, Edgar Schein, Daniel Levinson and Jeffrey Arnett. I have started from the teenage years because this is where we begin to see ourselves as individuals in the true sense of the word. The age ranges are only estimates – so take them with a grain of salt and focus more on the description of the life stage.

Asserting Independence and Trying Out New Things: 13—19 years old

From your early to late teens you increase your emphasis on the values of independence and experimentation. During this time, you experience all the chaos that goes with being a teenager. There is still the pull towards childhood, as well as the desire (and sometimes the push) towards adulthood. You are handed increased responsibilities and the parental ties are loosened. Expectations for you are higher and you begin to get the urge to make your own way in the world. You start to become more discerning and discriminating; and you assume a more stable character.

This is a time for fun, innovation and excitement. You meet new friends, join new groups and discover exciting ways of engaging with the world. You find mentors, teachers and guides. You learn through books, art, music or people. Your hope and enthusiasm play centre-stage. You begin to realise that you can fit in and stand out at the same time. In all your trials and challenges, you can and will make it. This is a time where you are active, alert, focused and becoming more and more capable. This is the time when you can really take note of the direction of the world – your world. It is your time to stand up and be counted. It's all about your ideas, your input, your influence, your say. Expect resistance: that is natural. Expect to be sneered at and undermined at times, too. These are the tools used by the people who are afraid. They use put-downs just because they can feel that you are on the way up! Faulty thinking causes them to fear your evolution.

This is a time to be okay with *some* rules, a time to respect those that have created a way that works for them. If you can see further than they can, you are supposed to. Each generation ought to be more advanced than the previous one. This is a time where you will need to channel your passion. Use your fire to get things done. Do creative things, play sport, play music, read books – do anything that captures your imagination in a good way. Do anything that feeds your mind or gives you more knowledge and skill. If you are driven to rebel, be a rebel with a *cause*. Find your flag to fly and do it proudly. Real passion is driven by compassion. Real revolution is driven by love. Real change comes by being the mirror of what you want to see.

Remember, this is a time to party! Set aside your fears and grab hold of the fun. Laugh until the tears come and your sides are about to burst. Spend time with your friends: among them are people you will treasure for the rest of your life.

Exercise: If you are 13—19 years old...
Here are some things to think about.

How can you have more fun?

_____
_____
_____
_____

What great hobby do you have that takes up lots of time?

_____
_____
_____
_____

What things are worth doing or worth improving?

_____
_____
_____
_____

What things really excite you?

_____
_____
_____
_____

What was the last occasion when you had a brilliant time?

_____
_____
_____
_____

How could you create another opportunity like that?

_____
_____
_____
_____

How often are you meeting up with your friends?

_____
_____
_____
_____

What are you doing to make your life better every day?

_____
_____
_____
_____

What do you want to stand for?

_____
_____
_____
_____

What do you want to do in your life?

_____
_____
_____
_____

How can you make this possible?

_____
_____
_____
_____

What skills do you need to make this happen?

_____
_____
_____
_____

- If you haven't laughed aloud at least once today, get out of your room!
- If you haven't been to at least one party this month, find one!

- You won't know unless you ask.
- Your job is to make it fun, fun, fun and then some. You can still do your bit.
- **Warning:** Seriousness is really an older person's disease. It can be contagious and it comes from forgetting the whole point of life. It can be avoided by ...?

Emerging Adulthood: 20–26 years old

It's never too late!
Didier Yves Drogba Tébily didn't get his first football contract until the age of twenty-one. It wasn't until the age of twenty-six that he joined Chelsea. Today, Drogba is thirty-four years of age and a world-class football player.

The challenges faced during this stage of life include moving out of the family home and trying to find a more permanent relationship with a romantic partner. At this stage, you are likely to make career direction choices and enter into something full-time. You might start college or an apprenticeship. You enter into a different social network and have to adjust position and rank from what you have been used to in school or within the family.

There is a whole new set of unwritten rules and norms that you have to learn in order for integration to take place. However, you also get a higher degree of choice and flexibility. The option is always there to leave one group and join another. As you move from teens to early twenties, things begin to stabilise and you are taken more seriously in work circles. You are no longer viewed as the teenager – you are a young man or woman – and you may already have recruits younger than you.

This stage of life is characterised by freedom and optimism: a view that no permanent decisions need be made about finance, career or life plans. You have time on your side. 'Sure, if I don't like it I can always try something else; there's plenty of time for all of that.' Your relationships progress: you may think about moving in, becoming engaged or getting married. You might even have thoughts and discussions about having children. You start to make more permanent lifestyle choices.

But this stage of life is different for you than it was for people a decade ago. Your transition from teen to young adult has a broader meaning. The traditional five-step life model is outdated and there isn't one massive move towards adulthood. You don't necessarily want to take on the roles expected by tradition. Maybe you shuffle and slouch a bit and you don't actually want to leave the nest at all. Maybe you keep mum and dad well in the frame and even call on them for advice, assistance or domestic duties. Does your mum still do your washing, even though you've been living in an apartment for years now?

Marriage is an option for you and single-parenting is a lifestyle choice. You've a liberal attitude to gay relationships – and some of your gay friends might even be married. Or maybe you haven't thought much about marriage and you've decided to focus on your career instead. You're probably in your first job and you know you can pursue lots of other things later on in your thirties: new careers, more education or having children.

Research from the US shows that one-third of you find a new place to live every year. Forty per cent of you choose to move back home with your parents at least once. You go through an average of seven jobs throughout your twenties. Two-thirds of you spend at least some time living with a romantic partner, without being married. If you do get married, you do this when you are 26–28 years old (the average used to be 21–23 years old).

Exercise: If you are 20—26 years old...
Here are some things to think about.

Do you want to be in a romantic relationship?

_____

_____

_____

_____

What are you doing to make sure that happens?

_____

_____

_____

_____

If you want to have children, what is the right age for you and your partner to be?

_____

_____

_____

_____

How much are you earning now?

_____

_____

_____

_____

How much would you need to live a good life?

_____

_____

_____

_____

What could you do to improve your prospects?

_____

_____

_____

_____

How will your actions today impact on your life in ten years' time?

_____

_____

_____

_____

Where would you like to be in fifteen years' time?

_____

_____

_____

_____

What would you do if you weren't doing what you are doing now?

_____

_____

_____

_____

- If you want to see the world, this could be the best time.
- If you want to have children, it might be time to be in a long-term relationship.
- It's time to look at the bigger picture!
- Settling down does not have to mean giving up or giving in.
- Commit to a relationship only if it adds to your life.
- Consider having children only when you are ready to trade some time.
- Bring all that you are into all that you are considering to do.
- Improvement works by addition, not subtraction.
- **Warning:** You really have got to ease off on the partying – just a bit.

Passing Through the Young Adult Stage: 27—31 years old

> **It's never too late!**
> **Harrison Ford** got his first real, paid supporting role at the age of twenty-nine. As a struggling actor, he paid his bills by doing carpentry. He is now known worldwide for his roles in the *Star Wars* and *Indiana Jones* movies.

At this stage, time becomes a pressing issue and you may start to do a review of your life. You'll ask, 'Is this what I want to be doing for the rest of my life? What do I want to get out of life? Where am I headed? Am I headed in the right direction?' As these questions are answered, you will either settle on a new direction or be happy with your current choices. You are more grounded about where you fit in and what your role is. You might decide to find a role outside the periphery or in opposition to it, but your role stabilises nonetheless.

Your thirties can be a considerable time for upheaval. Sometimes you hate the thoughts of being 'thirty-something'! You might have children by now and this brings a higher degree of commitment and time absorption. You might have to sacrifice certain pastimes for the sake of childrearing. The arrival of children imposes routine and may exclude (at least in part) your opportunity for new challenges.

You have a real urge to put down roots, if you haven't already done so. You begin to accept the likely permanency of the romantic relationship and you begin to bond more fully with the other person. You might sacrifice a degree of individuality for a more efficient and harmonious lifestyle. Roles and duties may cross over as you and your partner assume a common identity.

As you move to the end of this age range, you might consider becoming a mentor yourself. Busy and all as you are, you should keep an eye on the direction of your life. Time may be in high demand right now and *how you use it* will be up for review by you in another ten years' time. Right now, you have the vitality and ability to affect your life powerfully. With all that is happening to you in your work and home life, you need to take the time to think longer-term. You are hugely productive right now so you should ask, 'Am I producing the right things?'

This really is a wonderful time of life, so soak it up. Enjoy all the progress, the newness and the action. If you have children, it can only get better. If you are focused on your career, be sure that any offers or opportunities coming your way are measured against the other things going on in your life. If you are female, this really is the time to factor in whether you want to have children or not, so that you can plan ahead!

Exercise: If you are 27—31 years old...
Here are some things to think about.

List at least 5 things that you want to get out of life.

_____
_____
_____
_____

Where are you headed?

_____
_____
_____
_____

Are you headed in the right direction?

_____

_____

_____

_____

Is this what you want to be doing for the rest of your life?

_____

_____

_____

_____

How effectively are you managing your time?

_____

_____

_____

_____

Do you want to have children?

_____

_____

_____

_____

Are you happy in your relationship?

_____

_____

_____

_____

If you could change anything in your life, what would it be?

_____

_____

_____

_____

What stops you from doing that now?

_____
_____
_____
_____

What would happen if you did make the change?

_____
_____
_____
_____

What could you do now to improve your life considerably?

_____
_____
_____
_____

Do you need to learn more skills?

_____
_____
_____
_____

How can you plan that?

_____
_____
_____
_____

- Just because there is a rat race doesn't mean you have to take part.
- You have the time to make big changes now.
- The way you manage your time and priorities now will determine how you feel about yourself in ten years' time.
- Remember to take a breath and smell the roses!
- Family and fulfilment make it all worthwhile.
- **Warning:** Being 'thirty-something' is only difficult if you stop being flexible.

Personal and Professional Mastery:
32–42 years old

It's never too late!
Leonard Cohen did not release his first album until the age of thirty-two.

Andrea Bocelli always loved music but he did not start singing opera until the age of thirty-four.

Brendan Gleeson was thirty-four when he became a full-time actor. Considered now to be one of Ireland's greatest living actors, he has starred in movies such as *The Guard*, *Harry Potter*, *Braveheart*, *Mission Impossible 2*, *Artificial Intelligence*, *Gangs of New York* and *Troy*.

Anthony Burgess, who wrote *A Clockwork Orange*, published his first novel at the age of thirty-nine.

This is a life stage of relative stability and maturity. You have a strong sense of self. Though usually in a relationship, you are independent. Overall, you are satisfied with your life choices and direction. Your personal, social and professional roles are clearly defined and well established; and you have an active, positive participation in them. This is the time when your expertise and mastery is fine-tuned. You know what you are about, you know what you want and you are en route to that destination!

If you are enjoying yourself in this stage of life, you should still keep an eye on things. Nature is always producing change. Look after your health and wellbeing: it will serve you well in years to come. Keep an eye on the bigger picture and get ready to introduce change into your life. Start doing new things, since you have already mastered other things. This is all about growth, so keep on growing!

Exercise: If you are 32—42 years old...
Here are some things to think about.

Are you making sure you have the work–life balance right?

_____
_____
_____
_____

How much time have you spent with your family and loved ones this week?

_____
_____
_____
_____

Are you fully present when you are with your loved ones?

_____
_____
_____
_____

Is there anything you could do differently to show your partner that you love them?

_____
_____
_____
_____

What could you do to show your children that you love them?

_____
_____
_____
_____

How involved are you in the lives of your loved ones?

_____
_____
_____
_____

How up to date are your skills?

_____
_____
_____
_____

How fit are you?

_____
_____
_____
_____

How healthy are you?

_____
_____
_____
_____

What could you do to improve your health or fitness?

_____
_____
_____
_____

Are you happy with what you are doing?

_____
_____
_____
_____

If you could change anything, what would it be?

_____
_____
_____
_____

What stops you from making changes?

_____

_____

_____

_____

What would you do if you knew you could?

_____

_____

_____

_____

- Even when things are working well, keep on improving and keep on moving.
- Keep on defining and redefining what you are doing.
- Continue to find new ways to develop your creativity and mastery.
- Keep in mind that what works well can always work better.
- Remember: what works today may not be needed tomorrow.
- **Warning:** The only constant thing is change.

The Fabulous Forties

It's never too late!

Clint Eastwood directed his first film at the age of forty-one; and was the oldest person to win the Academy Award for Best Director.

Stan Lee, creator of _Spider-Man_, was forty-three when he began drawing his legendary superhero.

Jack Kirby was forty-four when he created the _Fantastic Four_ comic books.

Alan Rickman, of _Die Hard_ and _Harry Potter_ fame, got his first movie role at the age forty-six.

It is around this time that you are faced with your own mortality. Life gets reviewed again but, this time around, the time pressure weighs more heavily. You think in terms of finality and you question whether you have lived the life that you wanted to live. If the answer to this question is no, you wonder whether it is too late now to change it. You are faced with the issue of ageing and may begin to see the first signs of physical decline. The crow's feet and more permanent frown lines become harder to ignore! You reflect on your stage of life, and doing this can be a source of disruption, renewal and rebirth.

This is the time of the mid-life crisis! You may experience feelings of depression and loss because your 'youth' has passed. You may have feelings of fear. This may also be the time when your children first show signs of leave the nest. This can lead to a feeling of incompetence: the role of parent reduces to a large extent.

You may need a period of readjustment in the empty nest, as you return to being a couple without having any children around. You have a strong urge to pursue your own interests, while still keeping a connection with your life partner. Plans become more concrete and decisions about what is most important become clear. You actively integrate these decisions into action plans. You may deliberately withdraw from some social activities and engagements, so that your personal priorities can be restructured and you can establish a new life direction.

Exercise: If you are in your Fabulous Forties...
Here are some things to think about.

If there are things that you have not done but really think you should do, list them now.

_____
_____
_____
_____

List at least five things that you want to get out of life now.

_____
_____
_____
_____

Where is your life headed now?

_____
_____
_____
_____

Are you headed in a good direction?

_____
_____
_____
_____

Are you doing what you want to be doing?

_____
_____
_____
_____

What have you done to enjoy today?

_____
_____
_____
_____

What have you done today to improve someone else's day?

_____
_____
_____
_____

Are you happy with your relationship?

_____
_____
_____
_____

How can you improve it?

_____
_____
_____
_____

If you could change anything in your life, what would it be?

_____
_____
_____
_____

What stops you from doing that now?

_____
_____
_____
_____

What would happen if you did make this change?

_____
_____
_____
_____

What could you do now to improve your life considerably?

_____
_____
_____
_____

Do you need to learn more skills?

_____
_____
_____
_____

How can you plan that?

_____

_____

_____

_____

- Your health is important: look after it.
- Your life is important: take care of it.
- Your loved ones are important: spend more time with them.
- If you need to, speak about it.
- If you want to, change it.
- If you haven't done it, do it.
- **Warning:** Your time is your wealth. Where are you spending yours now?

The Question of Legacy: 49—65 years old

> **It's never too late!**
>
> **Ronald Reagan** was first elected to public office at the age of fifty-five, when he became Governor of California. He remains the oldest man to have served as US President.
>
> **Oscar Swahn** won a gold medal in the 1912 Olympics, becoming the best shooter in the world. He was sixty-four years old.
>
> **Colonel Sanders** began his Kentucky Fried Chicken franchise at the age of sixty-five.

Once the mid-life transition has been crossed, the dust from that trauma settles! At this time in your life, you can become incredibly productive. These years could actually be the most productive of your life. This is the time when you are at peak maturity and the issue of contribution raises high on the agenda. You may think about doing your greatest work or you may figure out a way of creating a legacy. The urge to give back becomes stronger and the ego gets pushed aside. You are less driven, less interested in competition and more interested in contribution. Personal values are reasserted and the concept of leaving the world a better place is more likely to come to the forefront. You may become involved in mentoring, stepping back and letting the younger ones have a go. You enjoy this process. This is a time of increased spiritual awareness and evolution for you. There is a higher degree of personal acceptance and a greater appreciation of children, partners and friends. You may even become a grandparent during this time.

Exercise: If you are 49—65 years old...
Here are some things to think about.

List a number of challenging projects you could take on, which would be beneficial to your personal life.

_____

_____

_____

_____

What could you do that would make you really proud of your life?

_____

_____

_____

_____

What do you want to be known and remembered for?

_____

_____

_____

_____

How do you want to give back?

_____

_____

_____

_____

How can you be of help?

_____

_____

_____

_____

Who would you like to nurture?

_____

_____

_____

_____

How do you want to do this?

_____

_____

_____

_____

Are you happy in your relationship?

_____

_____

_____

_____

How can you improve it?

_____

_____

_____

_____

If you could change anything in your life, what would it be?

_____

_____

_____

_____

What stops you from doing that now?

_____

_____

_____

_____

What would happen if you did make that change?

_____

_____

_____

_____

What could you do now to improve your life considerably?

_____

_____

_____

_____

Do you need to learn more skills?

_____

_____

_____

_____

How can you plan that?

_____

_____

_____

_____

- Time is your most valuable resource: use it wisely.
- Energy might be more scarce now, so build in a bit more time for recovery.
- Think strategically: your actual pace might not be your desired pace. It is pace nonetheless!
- **Warning:** Mental and physical capacities will only be maintained if you exercise them regularly.

Spiritual Embracement: 65 years and up!

It's never too late!

Frank McCourt published his first book, *Angela's Ashes*, when he was sixty-six. He later won the Pulitzer Prize for this book.

Peter Mark Roget had what is known as OCD (obsessive-compulsive disorder) and he found that the only thing that calmed him was making lists. When he retired from medicine at sixty-one, he spent his time making one huge, all-encompassing list; in doing so, he invented the thesaurus at the age of seventy-three.

Anna Mary Robertson Moses (Grandma Moses) is one of the biggest names in American folk art. She loved embroidery but, once her arthritis grew too painful for her to hold a needle, she decided to give painting a try. She was seventy-six.

Benjamin Franklin invented bifocals when he was seventy-eight.

Children's author **Mary Alice Fontenot** wrote almost thirty books, publishing multiple volumes in her eighties and nineties.

This is a time when you accept yourself and your life for what it is. This time of life can be characterised by cynicism or optimism. Your world view takes on a broader dimension to it and you recognise the passages that we all go through as part of being human. This period is typically characterised by a desire to hand on personal wisdom and insights to the younger generation. You consider wrapping things up and readying yourself for the onward journey. You may be ok with having some loose ends left to tie up – and you realise that not everything needs doing and not everything needs completing. You may hold on to life with a positive ferocity and resilience, all the while accepting that the time left may be limited. This gives you a freedom and a sense of appreciation that allows you to enjoy the simpler things more.

Exercise: If you are over 65 years old...

You've already thought about lots of things in your life. What wisdom would you care to share?

_____
_____
_____
_____
_____
_____

_____
_____
_____
_____
_____
_____
_____

Exercise: Think About Your Stage of Life

Look at the chart that follows and start this exercise at whatever section matches your current age. List five or more things you have done at this stage of your life. Listing what you have already accomplished reminds you how important it is that you live up to your greatest potential.

Now think about all the stages of life that are ahead of you. Think what it is you would like to have achieved by the end of your life, then mark out a path of necessary achievements along the way. You don't need a detailed plan – a selection of goals will do.

Keep this exercise with you as a constant reminder that you deserve to live an exceptional life!

In my teens, I have done/will do these five things and more...

_____
_____
_____
_____
_____

In my twenties, I have done/will do these five things and more...

_____
_____
_____
_____
_____

In my thirties, I have done/will do these five things and more...

_____

_____

_____

_____

_____

In my forties, I have done/will do these five things and more...

_____

_____

_____

_____

_____

In my fifties, I have done/will do these five things and more...

_____

_____

_____

_____

_____

In my sixties, I have done/will do these five things and more...

_____

_____

_____

_____

_____

In my seventies, I have done/will do these five things and more...

_____

_____

_____

_____

_____

In my eighties, I have done/will do these five things and more...

_____

_____

_____

_____

_____

In my nineties, I have done/will do these five things and more...

_____

_____

_____

_____

_____

Beyond that, I have done/will do these five things and more...

_____

_____

_____

_____

_____

And all so that I can look back and smile!

CHAPTER 11

The Rules of Engagement

So plastic is mind, so receptive, that the slightest thought makes an impression upon it. People who think many kinds of thoughts must expect to receive a confused manifestation in their lives. If a gardener plants a thousand kinds of seeds, he will get a thousand kinds of plants; it is the same in mind.

Ernest Holmes

There is a context in which all of what you have read so far must operate. This context does not appear to be manmade; not insofar as we can tell. It is a context that is bound by *principles* and it will operate regardless of what we do or what we think about it. It appears to be present; take it or leave it. To leave these considerations out of this book would be like asking you to run without being able to walk. In my own life I have noticed these principles. Over the years, they have become more widely known and popularised as 'laws', e.g. the Law of Attraction. Some of the other laws are not so well known but, in my opinion, are equally relevant. I have come across these principles in science, systems theory, psychology, physics and metaphysics. Many people want these laws to the true but they fail to apply them in the way that they are proposed.

It may be that my view of the world is unique to me. However, in my research, I have read many of the established (even classic) texts from many disciplines. Many of these books were written from a different mindset, at a time well before the personal development movement became the broad field of research it is today. But in so many of these texts, I see reflections of my own thinking. I believe that life as we know it is *what we make of it*. I also believe that there is a collective will and collective knowing and collective creating drive that is life; and each one of us is at the helm. We are the creators; and if we want things to get better we need to think collectively and respond collectively. If we do, the only limit we have is the point where we stop thinking. I am in total agreement with Einstein on all of this.

What follows in this chapter is an explanation of these laws. Read them, study them and look for their presence in your life. Then start to apply them, bit by bit, in your life – and see what happens.

1 The Law of Energy

We live in a world where everything is *connected*. There is an unseen dimension to reality. There is a structure behind all that we think, do and manifest. There is a force that frames our abilities: a malleable force; a force with laws. These laws are there for everyone to use. There is no criterion that excludes you from putting these laws to use in your life. Crucially, knowledge of these laws is useless unless you put them into practice. Those people who do make the shift become elevated from the norms of the ordinary to the realm of the extraordinary.

2 The Law of Vibration

The Law of Vibration states that 'nothing rests; everything moves, vibrates and travels in circular patterns'. In 1905 Albert Einstein proved that *all* matter, when broken down into its purest form, is simply *energy* vibrating at different frequencies. The lower and slower the vibration, the more solid the matter (and vice versa). The same can be said of emotions. Anger, fear, grief, anxiety and despair are the emotions that vibrate at the lower frequencies. Love, joy, happiness, appreciation and gratitude vibrate at higher, faster frequencies. The higher and faster the vibration, the more *power* it holds. Science has proven that energy cannot die; it can only be transformed. By its very nature, energy must go forward or backwards. It cannot stand still. In life, you cannot stand still: you must continue to move forward in line with the natural flow.

3 The Law of Evolution

Each of us has an inbuilt desire to improve, develop, become more, be more, have a greater impact and be better. This is a natural drive. It is as it should be. Many of the background tensions in our minds come from the frustration, boredom and lack of fulfilment that comes from ignoring this natural impulse. Human beings are the only species that get to *choose* whether they meet their full potential: all other life forms are simply driven towards it.

4   The Law of the Mind

This law states that mind exists everywhere and in everything. This mind, which includes your own, has the ability to exert influence on many things. The mind can generate and receive thoughts. The mind is that part of us that is non-local. It can be in more than one place at the one time. Have you ever physically come home from work but left your mind at work? This is an example of the mind being in two places at once. Remember also that the mind is weakened when its attention is splintered. This is why the ability to maintain the discipline of focus is so important. There are four levels of mind:

The Conscious Mind

Your conscious mind is your logical, rational, analytical, planning mind. It is often called your 'left brain'. It is the mind that you use to deliberately do things. If you decide to scratch your head, that comes from your conscious mind. The conscious mind makes you aware of what is happening to you and around you via sensations, perceptions, memories, feeling and fantasies. The conscious mind also acts as a filter and determines what is acceptable and unacceptable; and what is true or false. When you watch a movie, it is your conscious mind that tells you that this is not real: it is just make-believe.

This is the part of your mind responsible for short-term memory. These memories aren't immediately conscious but can be made conscious in an instant through conscious intention. For example, if I ask you what you just ate, you can easily pull that into your awareness quite quickly through the use of short-term memory. The conscious mind is selective and can only pay attention to a few things at a time (approximately 5–7 things) before it has to hand over responsibility to the subconscious mind.

The Subconscious Mind

Often referred to as your 'right brain', the subconscious mind is the part of your mind responsible for feelings, intuition, imagination and creativity. Your subconscious mind is the storehouse for all that has ever happened to you in your life. Your memories, habits, beliefs, values and all the automatic functions of your body are controlled from here. This is the mind that makes your heart beat. This is the part of you that can connect to infinite mind, universal intelligence or, as scientists call it, 'the unified field': the part of us that is connected to everything else.

The Collective Mind

The collective mind or collective consciousness is made up of the combined thoughts, imaginings and ideas of the entire planet. It is what we call 'reality'.

The Infinite Mind

The infinite mind or super conscious mind is the 'one mind', the 'all' that makes up the whole. The infinite mind is the invisible intelligence: omniscient, omnipresent and all-knowing. It is the mind that moves all things into being. It has been referred to as the 'first cause'. Some of you will choose to call it 'God'.

5   The Law of Free Will

Each of has the freedom to *choose* how we think about and react to the world around us. Ideally, this ought to translate into each of us having the freedom to do, be and go where we choose. Obviously, this is not the case for everyone. Many of us who are actually fortunate enough to have that freedom fail to claim it fully. Your freedom to choose gives you power over your life direction and expression. It is something to be explored, treasured and expressed. With this freedom comes the responsibility of being accountable for all your actions.

6   The Law of Manifestation

Everything starts out as a thought. Thought is the purest form of energy. Thinking is the act of tuning in to a particular frequency, possibility or option. The more you tune in, the more of it you get. There are as many options and possibilities as there are thoughts. Creative thought comes from or through your subconscious mind. We often refer to this type of thinking as 'thinking with your gut' or 'intuitive thinking'. These thoughts *create your reality*. Your ability to make your thoughts manifest comes down to a few simple things: the strength of your intention, the quality of your imagination, the power of your focus, and your self-belief. Get these right and the world is your playground!

Your ability to connect and engage all of your thinking is dependent on your relationship with your subconscious. You can enhance your connection by reflection, meditation, altered states of consciousness and hypnosis. Our intuition arises out of our subconscious mind and manifests itself as a push–pull system guiding us towards or away from certain actions that will either enhance or diminish our lives. This is the voice that knows. It is always correct. It processes all the possibilities that our conscious mind cannot.

You can increase your awareness of your intuitive abilities through meditation, prayer or relaxation – anything that allows you to quieten the busy, conscious mind and enter into a more reflective state.

You can release intuitive insight by feeding your subconscious with clear visual details of your goals.

You can allow your intuition to guide by becoming reactive and responding to what the mind presents at any given time. This is called 'living in the moment'. This requires that you increase your awareness of your internal responses to your external environment.

Be cautious about casting judgments or criticisms, or debating the apparent illogic of the push–pull system inside you. It has logic and it has a direction; it sees a bigger picture that you have planted but it is going on a route that you do not have consciousness awareness of yet. Remember: it is like a satellite navigation system in that it is continuously self-correcting. So, even if you make a mistake and go off course, it can bring you back to your goal. The quickest route for you to achieve this is to remind yourself of the bigger picture of where you are headed and you can do that by the simple process of reflection.

Every thought causes a physical reaction: angry thoughts stimulate your adrenal glands; anxious thoughts affect your pulse, heartbeat and stomach, etc. Thoughts can be accepted, rejected or replaced by higher forms of thought. You are free to think whatever you like. You are also free to respond to the thoughts of others however you like.

7 The Law of Desire

You may have heard this expression: 'You'll get what you want if you want it bad enough.' *Passion aids creation.* If you want something, you need to experience the feelings that go with already having it. When you flood your mind with the idea of the thing in detail, this activates your subconscious mind so that it takes it on board and drives all of your behaviour towards it. The more you remind yourself of it, the more it becomes hardwired into your brain as habit. You no longer need to think about it as it has become automated by your subconscious. You have tuned the channel and the frequency is set at the permanent 'on' position, taking you towards your goal with each wave.

8 The Law of Focus

This law echoes the yogic philosophy that states that where focus flows, energy follows. Whatever you place your attention, you place your energy; and the more you focus on it, the more energy it receives. Your energy is translated into thoughts, words, emotions and deeds; and this causes all of your experiences. This law further states that whatever you focus on, you also *become*. Basically, you are what you think about most often. It stands to reason that if our focus is splintered, if we are paying attention to too many things at once, our energy gets dispersed and that directly impacts our results. It makes sense to make an obsession of the things that are most important to you!

9 The Law of Distraction

For reasons of evolution, you are drawn towards the new, the different and the unusual. This ensures that you continue the process of learning, developing and growing. In turn, this ensures your survival in an ever-changing world.

However, there is a downside to this. If you have ever attempted to get something done and noticed that your attention was constantly being drawn away from it, then you have experienced this law at work! Let's say that, as I first type this paragraph, I notice a book in my peripheral vision. It is written by a good friend of mine, Paul Boross, and it is called *The Pitching Bible*. I stop for a moment and think to myself, 'I must ring Paul.' Then I think, 'I need to finish reading that book.' At this point, I am distracted from my own writing. Now I have many choices: I could stop what I am doing, I could pick up the phone to speak with Paul, I could read more of his book, etc. The reason my attention is drawn is because of the activity of a part of my brain called the reticular activating system. This is the part of the brain that selectively feeds my conscious brain with information that I have previously input as being of significant value to me. So my brain is trying to help me by reminding me, which is a good thing; but I am also aware that if I stop what I am doing now, that will be a bad thing. I am left with the choice and that choice will determine whether I achieve my goal of finishing my book on time. There is a reason why you have a conscious and subconscious dimension to your mind – and they complement each other. In my case, my conscious mind (my 'head') says that I should continue what I am doing; and my subconscious mind (my 'heart') trusts that I will be reminded again and again until it is done. For this I am grateful: I thank my mind and move on. Catch up with you some other time, Paul!

10 The Law of Cause and Effect

The Law of Cause and Effect states that every action has a corresponding reaction. You reap what you sow. You get back what you put in. Nothing happens by chance: there is an active force behind everything. Just because the action may not be visible, does not mean that it is not there. In the bigger picture, spirit is the cause and life is the effect. To understand this principle fully, you need to realise that your thoughts, emotions, words and deeds – and the motivations, desires and intentions *behind* each of these things – are considered to be actions. This is why we say that thoughts are things. This law is often called the Law of Karma.

11 The Law of Tension/Release

Life is like a pendulum: it swings between two extremes and what happens to you may be at either extreme or somewhere in between. Field theory demonstrates how the pursuit of a goal produces a *tension* in the person seeking it. All tension is followed by a *release*. In an ideal situation, this release happens after the goal has been achieved. This is not always the case, though: if the tension is too high, you may become overwhelmed and the release may happen beforehand. If it does, you need to take this as a marker on the journey. Going back to the beginning is not the route: that will only create more of the tension that has already reached its peak. The Law of Tension/Release states that everything vibrates and moves to certain rhythms. These rhythms establish seasons, cycles, stages of development and patterns. If a release has occurred, a cycle has been completed. But just because a cycle has been completed, that does not mean that you can't still achieve your goal.

12 The Law of Requisite Variety

What is needed is a newly refined sense of direction. Behavioural flexibility will allow you to hold on to your goal while changing the route towards it. Think of a fitness regime or diet you may have been on at one point; now think about how many times you said to yourself that you ought to go back to that. For your life to progress, there is no going back; you can only move forward. Depending on your sorting preference (sameness or different), you need to do something new, something different, or else add more of something to what you have already been doing. Either way, you must do something extra or different to move forward with grace.

13 The Law of Polarity

Life has an apparent dual dimension to it: night and day; good and bad; yin and yang; male and female, etc. Crucially, the elements of each pair combine and they are actually part of the one thing. The Law of Polarity states that everything is on a continuum and everything has an opposite. You can't have one without the other. Everything has its flip side. Everything is in contrast with its opposite. Therefore, you cannot know happiness if you have not experienced sadness. You cannot have light without the darkness. You cannot experience success without knowing failure. Every person has a male and female aspect to them. To negate one is to create an imbalance in the system. Both of these aspects need to be brought into balance and allowed to co-exist.

Knowledge of this law can help you to deal with challenging times. You must realise that adversity is directly connected (by way of contrast) to prosperity. So, if you are facing adversity, it means you are within swinging distance of prosperity. Keep the faith!

14 The Law of Expansion and Growth (Abundance)

The natural direction of life is towards abundance. Nature leans towards evolution, expansion and growth. We are like butterflies: given the right conditions, we can transform, expand, grow and become something much bigger and much more beautiful than our humble beginnings. In 1985, Bob Geldof wanted to start a movement to feed the starving people of Ethiopia. Little did he know that his goal of £1 million would grow into a £250 million manifestation and set the stage for one of the largest broadcasts of all time, which put 1.9 billion people across 150 nations into action. This is what is possible when the Law of Expansion is at work.

It is important to keep in mind the term 'expansion'. The expansion of an unspoken idea, more specifically *your* idea, may not be confined to your own direct action. Have you ever been thinking about a person and, before you know it, they pick up the phone and ring you? Have you ever wanted something only to find that someone offers that same thing to you seconds later? Have you ever had a thought and, as soon as you verbalise it, someone in your company tells you that they were just that minute thinking that exact same thing? These are all examples of the Law of Expansion at work. This gives legitimacy to the idea that 'thoughts are things'. You are not the only vehicle of your desires and dreams; other people can unconsciously align with them and carry them out, too. It is not always necessary to verbalise what you want: a thought with enough intention behind it will often do that for you.

15 The Law of Attraction and Reflection

This law states that *like attracts like*: things that resonate on the same frequency attract one another. The Law of Attraction is constant: there is no 'off' button. Whatever you think about, you are drawing this closer towards yourself. The Law of Attraction states that all thoughts have power and all thoughts exert influence. Therefore, the quality of your results in life will be determined by: your thoughts first; then your beliefs; your state of mind; your behaviours; your emotions; and naturally, your actions. The implications for this are huge! This emphasises that the quality of your attention will determine the results you are getting long before you actually get down to the business of doing anything about it. Think of the implications then for the things that you allow into your mind on a daily basis. Think about how your daily dose of news affects your mind. Think of the documentaries you watch that are all about crime, corruption and the darker side of life. These all impact your thought processes and leave imprints in their wake. Imagine then the *signal that is being sent out* as you *engage* with these things. That is a sobering thought, indeed.

16 The Law of Dominant Effect

The level of intent exists as a creative force; it is distinct from desire and decision. Wishful thinking, desire-based thinking or goal-setting thinking alone will get you nowhere. It all boils down to the level of *intent* that is driving the thought. So if you like the idea of something and decide that you are going to create a plan to get it, it will only happen if you fully sign up for it in your mind.

This is where the concept of intent comes into NLP; we call it 'congruency'. In order for something to happen, you need to align all your energies towards it so that it can gather momentum. You need to eat, drink and sleep it. You need to see it, hear it, feel it, believe it, be ready for it, and act on it – and all of this as if it has already been done!

You 'act as if' while you wait for the 'as if' to become manifest in the physical world. Once you have committed to this, only then can you trust enough to *let go*. You can do this now because the intention has taken on a life of its own and you need to put no further tension onto it. It has now moved to the actualisation phase, which means that it all becomes easy. The only effort it requires is to see it as already fully completed in your mind's eye.

Obviously, the quality of your internal representation of this will determine the level, quality and rate at which the thing will become manifest. Your mind is the tuning template from which all things come. It is the artist's palette – every sweep and curl of the brush is a message to the universe. This is why it makes sense to improve your sensory skills. It is like the creation of all great works of art: it makes sense to enter into the silence, embrace the stillness and wrap yourself in calm while you conjure up new and beautiful treasures that you have yet to experience. And again, as with all great works of art, one attempt is rarely enough. You need to revisit your creation through reflection and meditation, and continue to add in extra touches to enhance it. Once this is done, free yourself to do other things. In this way, you can return with fresh eyes every time you revisit your pending creation.

17 The Law of Substitution

The Law of Substitution states that your conscious mind can hold only one thought at a time, and that you can substitute one thought for another. Since we can choose what that thought will be at any given moment, it is essential that we remove habitual negative thoughts and replace them with positive, life-enhancing ones. We can do this first by using thought-stopping techniques. (If you read my first book, *The Happiness Habit*, you will know all about the STFU mantra!) Then we follow by filling the void with well-formed, positive, self-affirming statements. Start small and allow the habit to build over time.

18 The Law of Belief

Seeing is believing. Believing is seeing. Whatever you believe, you will see. Whatever you see is dependent on your beliefs. Whatever you expect, you will get. Belief is the cornerstone of manifesting. However, if the belief is absent there is no amount of visualisation that will produce your goals. If you want to achieve a goal, you must really *believe* that you are deserving and worthy of it. Sometimes you need to rebuild confidence or work on self-esteem before being able to claim your dreams.

Many of the goals we set for ourselves remain just that: goals, not achievements. The reason for this is our tendency to sabotage ourselves on various levels. There are times when we proceed before a solid belief has been established. This means that there is still a limiting self-belief causing the obstacle. You need to address this to allow yourself to get past it. No amount of positive thinking, wishful thinking or fantasising will change that. You need to address the core issue at hand. If you have not yet changed within, you cannot expect to see the change on the outside. Perhaps there is a fear holding you back. Behind that fear there is a belief. You know what has to happen Feeling a certain amount of tension is quite natural. All great goals require a level of tension in order to hold your focus. The tension will reduce as you act in accordance with your intuitions.

19 The Law of Perception

The Law of Perception states that your reality is affected and shaped by your past experiences. But just because your past affects your present, it need not determine your future. This law states that higher vibrations consume and transform lower ones. Since your mind resonates at a frequency that transmits all of what is in your mind, it makes sense to build newer, stronger, more self-enhancing *experiences* that will outshine and drown out the effects of the negative frequencies. Change is essential for progress: without it, all we do is repeat previously stored life scripts and recordings in a different setting.

20 The Law of Resistance

This law states that whatever you resist will persist. If you push up against life, it will push back. If you open up to going with the flow (thereby reducing your resistance), things will move in the direction you want. You may have heard this statement: 'That which you fear most will come to pass.' It appears in the Bible (Job 3:25) as: 'For the thing which I fear comes on me, That which I am afraid of comes to me.' Buddha said something similar: 'It is your resistance to what is that causes your suffering.'

Now put these statements in the context of 'fighting the fear', 'pushing the envelope', 'struggling on', etc. There is a big difference between *facing* your fear and *fighting* your fear. Facing your fear allows you to accept it and, once you do this, removes the resistance around it. In that way, you can overcome it. However, fighting your fear is like fighting fire with fire: all you get is more of the same. That is not a solution; that is simply an expansion. Think of the metaphor of 'standing your ground' and what happens when you do this.

21 The Law of Correspondence

Change is an inside job. Life is a mirror and what you see is your own reflection. Your outer world is a projection of your inner world. All that you experience on the outside corresponds to your dominant patterns of thinking. If you want to change or improve anything in your life, you must begin by changing the inner aspects of your mind. This is what Mahatma Gandhi meant when he said: 'Be the change that you want to see in this world.' If you want to live an exceptional life, you need to create exceptional experiences inside yourself first. You need to improve your internal architecture. This book will help you to do that. Once the foundations are reset, then you can imprint more effectively. The imaginings and imprints that you conjure up can then become the instructions that command the reality you are about to experience. How far you go is up to you.

Evidence of the Law of Correspondence can be found in your relationships. Think about following saying: 'You teach people how to treat you.' If you extend this thinking to include your health, wealth and success, the implications are as huge as the responsibility. Once you begin to believe that this law could be true, your responsibility for personal mastery and change becomes much greater.

22 The Law of Habitual Action

Many people know what to do in life but few get around to actually doing it. Knowledge of what to do is only potential power. By itself it has no real power. Knowledge is only powerful when applied to *action*. Reading this book will give you knowledge. Applying that knowledge has the power to help you shift swiftly from the ordinary to the extraordinary. The application of knowledge completes the cycle of energy.

Goethe said: 'Knowing is not enough; we must apply. Willing is not enough; we must do.' Bruce Lee was another person very aware of the power of repetition. He once said that he would not fear the man who has practised 10,000 kicks once, but he would fear the man who has practised one kick 10,000 times. Doing a thing once or twice is rarely enough: you need to make a habit of doing certain things. However challenging or tedious this approach may appear, it is the path to the extraordinary.

Once you get started, it becomes easier to keep going. To do this, you need to learn how to form new habits. Old habits produce limitations that, left unchallenged, can impede progress. To form new habits you need to open your mind and challenge your existing belief sets effectively. As you do that, you also need to replace the old habits with stronger, more empowering assumptions. It is in doing this that you can achieve your goals.

23 The Law of Detachment

The Law of Detachment requires a strong degree of faith or belief in the idea that 'the universe will provide'. Abraham Maslow stated that, once a goal has been formulated in your mind, it is necessary (paradoxically) to detach from it emotionally. Remember: this does not mean that you detach from it behaviourally! In order for your goal to happen, you need to hold some active part in it. What Maslow actually pointed to is the need for a shift from the proactive mode of pushing to achieve, to the reactive mode of expecting to receive, all the while being ready to be prompted into action.

This means looking for and responding to the signs and opportunities that are being presented to you in every moment. Once the mind has signed up, it is simply a matter of helping the goal to show up by reacting to the nudges that will inevitably come your way. Your trust in either your mind, in God or in the universe is the acceleration that makes all of this happen. It may seem contradictory but the Law of Detachment requires that, once you have set your intention you need to hand it over to your subconscious mind to begin the process of bringing it into the physical dimension. Subconscious thinking is higher-order thinking because it includes more of your brain in the process. This is the mind of feelings, imagination, intuition and habit. A goal, thought or intention handed over to this level of mind will be taken as automatic, so it will operate in the background. This is the mind that will nudge you in the right direction through synchronicity and apparent coincidence. Therefore, once the intention is set, it is best to leave the subconscious to put it in motion.

You will find that, every so often, a thought will come and a flash of inspiration will shoot into your awareness. When that happens, your job is to acknowledge it and offer gratitude to it in the knowledge that your mind is serving you. If it has led you to an action, then do not question it – just act on it. This is progress towards your goal and your mind is guiding you. If the universe speaks to you, see it what way you will. Once you have responded to it, detach from it again: your brain will continue to work away, below your everyday level of awareness, in order to achieve your goal. Know that when your reaction is needed, it will be made known to you. Just remain open. Be willing to trust that this process has only *your* intention at heart – so go with it and enjoy it.

24 The Law of Gratitude

Many of us approach life from the perspective of what we can get from it. We are so tuned in to that frequency that we do not remember to stop and see what we have *already* received and achieved. In our youth, we tend to race forward in full warrior mode: pillaging, plundering and accumulating all that we can, as if abundance was scarce and there was no tomorrow. In doing this, you can achieve many things and that is good; but *greatness* happens when you can stop and take stock of what you already have. It goes without saying that you have been instrumental in bringing what you have into your life; yes, there may have been blood, sweat and tears shed for it but you did succeed; you have it; you have achieved it; enjoy it!

Let me also invite you to take a closer look to see that there are so many things you have that have come *easily* to you. It may be your friendships, family, partner or children. Think about the simple things that make your life better: your phone, the internet, the clothes on your back, the last meal you ate … Look around and take stock of all the good things that are in your world. You have many things that you didn't have to put conscious effort into attaining. These things are there for your benefit; simply appreciate them.

When you bring your focus as objectively as you can to all that you have in your life right now, this creates space for gratitude. Once you do this, you activate the Law of Gratitude. The law is based on the fact that what goes around comes around. If you project that feeling of genuine gratitude, it will come back to you with added benefits. When you operate from the attitude of gratitude, your mind builds the pattern. Then you start seeing *more* things you can be grateful for. This creates good feelings and a positive perspective. If you focus on the positive things in your life, more positive things will then be attracted to you. Demonstrate and express your appreciation. Begin to give back. Then the more you give, the more you will receive. The more you help others, the more you help yourself. It's a real win-win scenario.

Putting the Laws into Practice

Read about these laws many times. Take a copy of the summary below and bring it around with you. Pay attention to what is happening around you – and try to see how the laws are operating in your life.

Once you become familiar with these laws, you will realise that you have to incorporate them into your thoughts and into everything you do. Learn to master these laws and your life will be truly extraordinary!

	Law	Meaning
1	The Law of Energy	*Everything is connected.*
2	The Law of Vibration	*Nothing rests; everything moves.*
3	The Law of Evolution	*You are designed to grow.*
4	The Law of the Mind	*Mind is in everything. It can generate and receive thoughts.*
5	The Law of Free Will	*You choose your thoughts and behaviours.*
6	The Law of Manifestation	*Your thoughts create your reality.*
7	The Law of Desire	*Your desire gives strength to your thoughts.*
8	The Law of Focus	*Energy flows where focus goes.*
9	The Law of Distraction	*Distraction will happen.*
10	The Law of Cause and Effect	*You reap what you sow.*
11	The Law of Tension/Release	*All tension is followed by a release.*
12	The Law of Requisite Variety	*Change your behaviour, not the goal.*
13	The Law of Polarity	*You can't have one thing without its opposite.*

	Law	Meaning
14	The Law of Expansion and Growth (Abundance)	*A thought that takes root will expand.*
15	The Law of Attraction and Reflection	*You attract what you are.*
16	The Law of Dominant Effect	*The strongest thought wins.*
17	The Law of Substitution	*Your mind can only hold one thought at a time.*
18	The Law of Belief	*Believing is seeing.*
19	The Law of Perception	*Reality is shaped by your past experience.*
20	The Law of Resistance	*What you resist persists.*
21	The Law of Correspondence	*Life is a mirror of your internal world.*
22	The Law of Habitual Action	*Effort produces results.*
23	The Law of Detachment	*You must trust the universe to provide.*
24	The Law of Gratitude	*Appreciation breeds abundance.*

CHAPTER 12

Modelling Excellence

> *Sow a thought and you reap an action; sow an act and you reap a habit; sow a habit and you reap a character; sow a character and you reap a destiny.*
>
> **Anonymous**

I hope that you have enjoyed what this book has to offer and I believe that there are so many things you can take from it on your journey towards the extraordinary. You really can change the course of your life once you put the lessons from this book into practice. I hope that you will work to perfect and master all of what has been explored but, at the same time, I realise that your life is busy and you have things to do and places to go. One thing I learned early on in my own journey was that it takes time to give a book a good read. I ask that you give this one your best shot! I remember hearing somewhere that you don't know a thing until you have heard it at least *seventeen* times. You might not read this book seventeen times but I am sure you have realised already that working on improving your life takes a *lot* of practice. Practice is the thing that produces results. In this chapter, we will examine some practices that can help you on your journey.

Modelling Excellence

NLP is known as the study of excellence. It is all about *modelling excellence*. In this last chapter, you will learn crucial tools for modelling excellence in your own life. These tools will help you to do your own research so that you can make your own progress.

There may come a time when you would like to learn a new skill from someone that you know. Every day you are surrounded by amazing people who have learned how to do exceptional things. Often, you'll be curious to know just how exactly they did that. Because of the nature of the mind and its inclination towards the formation of habits, if you ask a person how they do something extraordinary they might not be able to communicate it to you. You might get a handful of tips, perhaps you'll hear some life advice about never giving up, but you may not get the explanation you are really after. This is because the person has a level of *unconscious competence*. They no longer know how it is that they do what they do: this is buried in the deeper recesses of their mind. It is no longer a conscious thought, so you will have to take a different approach if you want to model their excellence.

Modelling is the process involved when you create useful maps of someone else's experience or behaviour with the purpose of learning a particular skill (or set of skills). Modelling is designed to look at all the levels of activity that a human being engages in when performing a certain task. It takes into account both conscious *and* unconscious activities. If you want to learn how a person performs a certain function, you need to go deeper than the surface structure, which is their conscious knowledge of their activity. You need to investigate the *beliefs* that are present in order for them to engage in the activity. You need to look at the thinking that lies *behind* the actions, as well as the feelings and behaviours that go with the actions. Behaviours include verbal and non-verbal cues. So if you want to model something another person does, you need to observe that person while they are doing it. You need to see them running the activities live in front of you. Watch the cook in the kitchen, so to speak.

Asking Questions so that You Can Model Excellence

In reality, it is not always possible to do a live observation of an extraordinary person performing their task. So how can you discover what extraordinary people do in order to model them yourself? You can ask questions. NLP developer Robert Dilts has come up with a model based on six Neurological Levels of Learning. Each level offers valuable insight into the reasoning, motivation and methodology used by a person in determining their ability to perform the skill. I have combined the work of Dilts with that of other NLP developers (including Richard Bandler and David Gordon) to provide you with a set of questions you can ask to discover how extraordinary people do extraordinary things.

The questions will help you to uncover information that would otherwise have been unavailable to you. Let's examine the levels and the questions below. Bear in mind that, while the levels are presented in hierarchical form, this structure does not have to be followed in practice. The levels are interdependent, but the higher up you go, the less flexibility there is in the system.

Environment

The base level of questioning involves asking about a person's environment. This is the where the activity takes place. If you want to model a boxer, you need to look at their environment. At a micro level, this means the boxing ring and its surroundings; at a macro level, this extends to include their neighbourhood, state and country. The more information you can gather, the better – as long as it is relevant to the task that you want to study.

Questions about *environment* include:
- What has to be present when you are doing this?
- Where do you do this?
- When do you do this?

Behaviour

If you want to examine a boxer's behaviour, it is not enough to look only at their behaviour in the boxing ring. You need to examine their behaviour before a fight, during a fight and after a fight. You want to know how they behaved when they lost a fight and when they won a fight. You want to know their every move. You want to know what they did to make a left uppercut or a right-hand jab. You want to know everything.

Questions about *behaviour* include:
- What is it that you do?
- What do you mean by that?
- How do you know when you are doing it right?
- What do you do when things aren't going according to plan?
- What behaviours are evident when you are doing this?

Capacity

If you want to learn about a person's capacity, you must learn about their mind. In modelling a boxer, you need to know about their state of mind and their strategies. You want to know what goes through their mind when they are boxing. What do they say to themselves? What tone do they use? What is their sensory preference? When they prepare for a fight, do they use pictures, sounds or feelings? Do they use all of these things? What are the imperatives? What needs to be there for them in order for them to feel capable?

Questions about *capacity* include:
- How do you do what you do?
- What do you normally do?
- What makes it possible?
- What has to be there?
- What feelings are present?

Beliefs and Values

This is the *why* behind the person's actions. This is the force that gives them their passion. If you want to model a boxer, you want to know what it is that they believe. Do they believe they are the greatest? You want to know why they box. You want to know what is so important to them about boxing. You want to know why they wouldn't do something else instead.

Questions about *beliefs and values* include:
- Why do you do this?
- When you are doing this, what is important to you?
- What do you mean by that?
- What is important about that?
- Why is that important?

Identity

Once you understand the *why*, you need to know the *who*. If it's a boxer, you now know why they fight, but *who are they*? You want to know how they view themselves. You want to know if there is one identity for inside the ring and one identity for outside the ring. You want to know about all the roles they play in life.

Questions about *identity* include:
- Who are you?
- Describe who you are when you are doing this.
- Are you different at other times?

Spirituality

You want to know if the person is working to a higher calling. Most big achievers feel that they are. If it's a boxer, you want to ask them who they are doing it for. Is it for God? Is it for their nation? Is there another reason altogether? Usually, there is a higher purpose involved for people to make a big commitment.

Questions about *spirituality* include:
- What is the big picture behind all that you do?
- What do you believe in?

Once you have asked questions on all of these levels, you will be in a much better position to adapt and integrate some of those skills for yourself. The idea behind this is to gather as much information as possible, so that if you are going to try and replicate the person's behaviour, you are armed with as much detailed information as possible.

Remember: while modelling has its uses, it also has its limitations. Just learning how a person boxes doesn't mean that you automatically know how to box as well. You won't be able to do it just like them. However, you will be able to learn about their skills and *add them to your own*. This will improve your performance considerably.

Modelling is a fantastic tool and I suggest that you use it. There is so much more to it than can be covered in this chapter. If you want to learn more about it, read some of the work of Robert Dilts. It would also be worthwhile to check out a book called *Expanding Your World* by David Gordon and Graham Dawes.

The Four Stages of Competence

Keep in mind that, as you learn to master skills, you will go through different stages. There are four stages of competence.

Stage One: Unconscious Incompetence

This is the point where you have not yet noticed that there is a particular skill available that you do not understand or know how to do. Basically, you *don't know* that you don't know. Once you identify your lack of the skill, you move to the next stage.

Stage Two: Conscious Incompetence
Although you do not understand how to do the skill yet, you do recognise the knowledge deficit. You see the value of having this new skill. You may not get it right the first few times but that is just part of the learning process. You *know* that you don't know how to do it just yet.

Stage Three: Conscious Competence
As you get to apply your new skill, you realise that it calls for a lot of concentration. Now you *know* you know how to do it.

Stage Four: Unconscious Competence
After you have applied your skill a number of times, it becomes 'second nature' to you. As a result, the skill can be performed while doing something else and you may even be able to teach it to others at this stage. You no longer know *how* you know: you just can do it without thinking. It has become habit.

The Raikov Effect

Now it may be that you will identify someone who has a skill that you would like to acquire and perhaps you may not have the opportunity to interview or speak with them. If that is the case, you can always use the Raikov Effect. The Raikov Effect is a deep trance identification technique that gets you to use your imagination in order to learn a skill from someone else.

Exercise: Deep Trance Identification Technique

You need to close your eyes and relax for this process, so read the instructions first and memorise them before you begin. That way you will really be able to focus.

1. Choose your subject.
2. Use your imagination to pretend that you *are* your subject.
3. Now, do as they do; be as they are. Fill your imagination with the idea of being them.
4. If you want, you can make an image of them standing in front of you with their back to you. Then imagine yourself taking a step forward and stepping right into their body.
5. From this perspective, you can see through their eyes, hear through their ears and feel as they feel.
6. Take your time and fully immerse yourself in the experience.
7. Allow yourself to walk, talk and move like them. Engage all of your senses. Capture every minute detail that you can.
8. Learn from this experience. Stay aware and in tune to any insights that arise. Make a mental note of the thoughts, feelings and sensations that come to you as you allow yourself to go fully with this experience.
9. When you are done, allow yourself a moment to tune back in to your own body. If you like, see yourself stepping out of your chosen subject's body and stepping back into your own.
10. Then thank your subject and open your eyes.

You might think that this is a pointless exercise but don't dismiss it. This is how children learn a lot of the time. Have you ever seen them watch a video of a person dancing, for instance? It's as if they step inside the body of the other person and mirror their every move. They are utterly absorbed in the process and they learn from it.

My 'Train of Thought' Technique

I am no different from anyone else in that I have had my ups and downs in life. However, one thing that has always sustained me is my belief in the extraordinary. I come from ordinary beginnings but I have always believed in our ability to focus our minds and get them to work for us; this ability continues to fascinate me. It has delivered some really cool results in my own life and I know for certain that it can in yours.

I came up with this 'train of thought' technique and I have used it a lot throughout my life. I find it works really well just before I go to sleep for the night. Try it yourself.

1. The trick is to keep a level head when it comes to your internal world. Ground and centre first, in whatever way works for you. Take stock of the moment you are in. Separate yourself from the running thoughts in your mind for a moment; and just *be*.

2. The next step is to see things as they are, not as you want them to be. Whatever is happening, just make yourself aware of it without any impositions.

3. There is nothing for you to do in advance. Just stop right now and notice your surroundings. Take stock of your awareness. Become aware that you are aware.

4. From here, allow your thoughts to flow. Allow the commentary to run in your mind again. Engage with the feelings. Dive, steer and navigate. Adjust and alter whatever you feel needs attention. This allows you to delve deeper into your mind.

5. Work with your thoughts. Think of the scenario you want to create and run with it. Go straight for the victory; right to the end point.

6. Allow a positive feeling to build in your mind. It doesn't matter how weak it may be, once you can barely grasp a feel of it, you can work with it.

7. Once you have the positive feeling, keep going forwards and backwards into it. Repeatedly run your chosen scenario in your mind.

8. Every so often, you will be hit with an image that fills your mind. It may go as quickly as it arrives but that doesn't matter. As soon as you get a taste of it you know it is there, and it is just a matter of reworking things to get it to flash into your mind again.

9. When you feel you have engaged with your chosen scenario, turn on your side and trust that your subconscious will keep working on this throughout the night.

10. If you wake during the night, run the scenario again. This time add an internal commentary about how you want things to work out.

Conclusion

Most of my creative work is done in bed. It is there that I have spent many a night running through my goals in my mind. Doing this has confirmed for me that there is no end to the possibilities. I now know that if you can think it, you can bring it about. I have had very few days in my life that have been without challenge but every one of those challenges has produced dividends. I suspect that I have a deeper belief within me that requires those challenges of me; but I am fine with that because it lets me know I am alive.

I am in bed now as I type. Dawn has broken and I am getting that feeling that comes when you are close to your goal. It is a mixture of happiness and pride and anticipation. I know I'm almost there now but I don't know where all this will take me. Writing this book has been a challenge but it is one for which I am grateful. I have had to face some demons on the way; but that's life, isn't it? I have had to change direction. I have had to discard months of research in order to accept what my intuition was telling me. I have had to overhaul this entire book from cover to cover but I hope that it is all the better for it. I encountered a few roadblocks, certainly; but, of course, I can see now that they were opportunities that I just hadn't recognised. And now that everything is done, I hope you can see all the opportunities ahead of you.

There is so much to be excited about, passionate about. Passion is what will set your goal in motion. Logic is what will ground you. Intuition is what will guide you. Combine these things with some of the mental gymnastics you've learned in this book and you are truly ready to rock and roll! It is time to open the doors of opportunity and find out just how cool that software package between your ears really is.

When you decide to move beyond what you are accustomed to, when you set aside familiar patterns and courageously step into unknown realms, your life takes on a new dimension. Moments become magically transformed; a new light fills your awareness. The same world now holds a different meaning. The same words bring different feelings: you learn your new language. This language moves you from the ordinary to the extraordinary. You experience your life for what it is: an amazing complexity of combined sensory experiences.

You get to choose the spell that you cast on the invisible force that connects us. You get to weave your hypnotic dreams and pluck them from the ether. It is you who shapes and crafts and orchestrates the symphony that is your life. It will have ups and downs, thrills and spills, dramas and melodramas – but you are always the architect and it is your emotions that provide the foundation for all that you build.

There has to be an element of 'handing over' when you move towards the extraordinary. You must trust in the workings of the universe. You must trust that, in all that you do, there is a lesson waiting to be learned. It is not always the lesson you would have chosen, but it is always the one you actually need. It is my sincere hope that this book helps you to feel more connected to the greater part of you. I hope that you get to feel its full force in a positively extraordinary manner throughout your whole life. We are always experiencing what we have created. I hope that you come to understand that at a somatic level, at the level of feeling. What will you do with your knowledge? I hope you are happy to share it with anyone who wants a part of it. Your action will always be rewarded; this is simply how things work.

If you trustingly go with the flow, reality becomes less rigid and more flexible. All that you want becomes possible. There is a time for dreaming with both feet firmly fixed on this earth. This is the time. I hope you dream wildly. I hope you dream vividly. I hope you dream lovingly and respectfully. I hope you are prepared to give back to the Great Spirit who has nurtured your every breath. This is your world. Make it a great one.

Treat the earth and all that dwell thereon with respect.

Remain close to the Great Spirit.

Show great respect for your fellow beings.

Work together for the benefit of all humankind.

Give assistance and kindness wherever needed.

Do what you know to be right.

Look after the wellbeing of mind and body.

Dedicate a share of your efforts to the greater good.

Be truthful and honest at all times.

Take full responsibility for your actions.

Bibliography

Bandler, Richard, *Get the Life You Want: The Secrets to Quick and Lasting Life Change with Neuro-Linguistic Programming*, HCI, 2008.

Bandler, Richard, *Magic In Action*, Meta Publications, 1992.

Bandler, Richard, *Persuasion Engineering*, Meta Publications, 1996.

Bandler, Richard, *Richard Bandler's Guide to Trance-formation: How to Harness the Power of Hypnosis to Ignite Effortless and Lasting Change*, HCI, 2008.

Bandler, Richard, *Time for a Change*, Meta Publications, 1993.

Bandler, Richard and John Grinder, *The Structure of Magic I: A Book about Language and Therapy*, Science & Behavior Books, 1975.

Bandler, Richard and John Grinder, *The Structure of Magic II: A Book about Communication and Change*, Science & Behavior Books, 1975.

Bandler, Richard and Will McDonald, *An Insiders' Guide to Submodalities*, Meta Publications, 1989.

Barrios, Alfred, *Towards Greater Freedom and Happiness*, SPC, 1985.

Beck, Don Edward and Christopher C. Cowan, *Spiral Dynamics*, Blackwell Publishing, 1996.

Bhikkhu, Thanissaro and Geoffrey DeGraff, *Purity of Heart*, Metta Forest Monastery, 2006.

Buzan, Tony, *Buzan's Book of Genius*, Touchstone, 1994.

Buzan, Tony, *Make the Most of Your Mind*, Touchstone, 1984.

Charvet, Shelle Rose, *Words that Change Minds*, Kendall Hunt, 2010.

Colbert, Brian, *The Happiness Habit*, Gill & Macmillan, 2010.

Dilts, Robert, *Applications of Neuro-Linguistic Programming*, Meta Publications, 1983.

Dilts, Robert, *Changing Belief Systems with NLP*, Meta Publications, 1990.

Dilts, Robert, *Cognitive Patterns of Jesus of Nazareth, Dynamic Learning Publications*, Ben Lomond, 1992.

Dilts, Robert, *From Coach to Awakener*, Meta Publications, 2003.

Dilts, Robert, *Modeling With NLP*, Meta Publications, 1998.

Dilts, Robert, *Roots of Neuro-Linguistic Programming*, Meta Publications, 1983.

Dilts, Robert, *Sleight of Mouth: The Magic of Conversational Belief Change*, Meta Publications, 1999.

Dilts, Robert, *Strategies of Genius Volumes I, II & III*, Meta Publications, 1994–1995.

Dilts, Robert, *Visionary Leadership Skills: Creating a World to which People Want to Belong*, Meta Publications, 1996.

Dilts, Robert and Gino Bonissone, *Skills for the Future*, Meta Publications, 1993.

Dilts, Robert and Judith A. Delozier, *Encyclopedia of Systemic Neuro-Linguistic Programming and NLP New Coding*, NLP University Press, 2000.

Dilts, Robert and Todd Epstein, *Dynamic Learning*, Meta Publications, 1995.

Dilts, Robert and Todd Epstein, *Tools for Dreamers: Strategies of Creativity and the Structure of Innovation*, Meta Publications, 1991.

Eysenck, Michael and Mark Keane, *Cognitive Psychology*, Psychology Press, 2005.

Foer, Joshua, *Moonwalking with Einstein: The Art and Science of Remembering Everything*, Penguin Books, 2012.

Gordon, David and Graham Dawes, *Expanding Your World*, David Gordon, 2005.

Gosling, Sam, *Snoop*, Basic Books, 2009.

Grinder, John and Richard Bandler, *Frogs into Princes: Neuro Linguistic Programming*, Real People Press, 1979.

Grinder, John and Richard Bandler, *Patterns of the Hypnotic Techniques of Milton H. Erickson,* Cupertino, 1976.

Grinder, John and Richard Bandler, *Reframing: Neurolinguistic Programming and the Transformation of Meaning*, Real People Press, 1983.

Grinder, John and Richard Bandler, *Trance-Formations: Neuro-Linguistic Programming and the Structure of Hypnosis*, Real People Press, 1981.

Grinder, John and Richard Bandler, *Using Your Brain for a Change*, Real People Press, 1988.

Hill, Napoleon, *Think and Grow Rich*, Tribeca, 2012.

Johnston, Daniel, *Lessons for Living*, Dagali Press, 2001.

Lewis, Byron and Frank Pucelik, *Magic of NLP Demystified*, Metamorphous Press, 1990.

McCall, Richard, *The Way of the Warrior-Trader*, McGraw-Hill, 1997.

McNab, Peter, *Towards an Integral Vision*, Trafford Publishing, 2006.

Martin, G. Neil, Carlson, Neil R. and William Buskist, *Psychology*, Pearson, 2010.

Maslow, Abraham, *The Farther Reaches of Human Nature*, The Viking Press, 1971.

Masterson, Michael, *Ready, Fire, Aim: Zero to $100 Million in No Time Flat*, Wiley, 2008.

Meyer, Pamela, *Liespotting*, St. Martin's Press, 2010.

Milanovich, Norma J. and Shirley D. McCune, *The Light Shall Set You Free*, Athena, 1996.

Navarro, Joe, *What Every Body is Saying*, William Morrow Paperbacks, 2008.

Nierenberg, Gerard and Henry Calero, *How To Read a Person Like a Book*, Thorsons, 1980.

Rogers, Carl, *A Way of Being*, Mariner Books, 1980.

Rogers, Carl, *Carl Rogers on Personal Power*, Trans-Atlantic Publications, 1978.

Rogers, Carl and Peter D. Kramer, *On Becoming a Person*, Mariner Books, 1995.

Rowland, Ian, *The Full Facts Book of Cold Reading*, Ian Rowland Ltd, 2008.

Satir, Virginia, *Peoplemaking*, Souvenir Press, 1994.

Sheehy, Gail, *Passages: Predictable Crises of Adult Life*, Ballantine Books, 2006.

Shenk, David, *The Genius in All of Us: New Insights into Genetics, Talent, and IQ*, Anchor, 2011.

Straker, David, *Changing Minds in Detail*, Suque , 2010.

Sutphen, Dick, *Lighting the Light Within*, Valley of the Sun Publishing, 1987.

Suzuki, D. T. and Christmas Humphreys, *Essays in Zen Buddhism*, Grove Press, 1994.

Tay, Louis, 'Needs and Subjective Well-Being Around the World'. *Journal of Personality and Social Psychology* 101 (2): 354–365.

Tracy, Brian, *How the Best Leaders Lead*, AMACOM, 2010.

Tracy, Brian, *Maximum Achievement*, Simon & Schuster, 1995.

Wenger, Win, *Brain Boosters*, (Audio CD) Nightingale Conant, 2003.

Wenger, Win and Richard Poe, *The Einstein Factor*, Gramercy, 2004.

Irish Institute of NLP

Brian Colbert and Owen Fitzpatrick co-founded the Irish Institute of NLP (Neuro-Linguistic Programming) in 2001. Brian is the author of bestselling book *The Happiness Habit*. He is a much sought-after keynote motivational speaker and is well known for his appearances on national TV and radio and in print media. He is recognised as one of the top NLP Master Trainers in the world. Owen is known for his popular RTÉ television series *Not Enough Hours* and is also a world-renowned Master Trainer of NLP.

Owen and Brian are the only Master Trainers of NLP in Ireland. They are highly recommended by Dr Richard Bandler (co-founder of NLP) and the Society of NLP, the largest and oldest NLP training body in the world. They are known for their remarkable ability to work together seamlessly and with great humour. Their unique training style reveals their great friendship and ability to complement each other.

Since they founded the Institute, Brian and Owen have presented NLP seminars in Ireland, Europe and America. They provide certification programmes for NLP Practitioners, NLP Business Practitioners, NLP Master Practitioners and NLP Coaches; and they offer many Evening Workshops and Life-Enhancement Weekends.

Owen and Brian also offer corporate consulting and present in-house training to the corporate sector in the areas of communication, sales, motivation, stress management, creativity and business applications of NLP.

To learn NLP in Ireland or to make your life and business better, visit the Institute's website today (contact details overleaf).

Brian is also available for public speaking engagements or in-house consulting work.

Irish Institute of NLP
84 Sundrive Road
Kimmage
Dublin 12
Ireland
Tel: +353 (0)1 490 2923

Websites:	www.briancolbert.ie
	www.nlp.ie
	www.thehappinesshabit.ie
	www.owenfitzpatrick.com
E-mail:	theresa@nlp.ie
Facebook:	/briancolbertnlp
	/thehappinesshabit
Twitter:	@IINLP
App:	Digipill